THE WILD YEAR

THE WILD YEAR

Jen Benson

Aurum

First published in 2022 by Aurum,
an imprint of The Quarto Group.
The Old Brewery, 6 Blundell Street,
London, N7 9BH, United Kingdom.

www.Quarto.com/Aurum

A catalogue record for this book is available from the British Library.

ISBN: 978-0-7112-6730-5
Ebook ISBN: 978-0-7112-6732-9
Audiobook ISBN: 978-0-7112-6733-6

1 2 3 4 5 6 7 8 9 10

Cover design by Anna Morrison
Typeset in ITC Berkeley Oldstyle by SX Composing DTP, Rayleigh, Essex, SS6 7EF
Printed and bound by CPI Group (UK) Ltd, Croydon, CR0 4YY

AUTHORS NOTE

The stories in this book reflect the author's recollection of events. Some names, locations, and identifying characteristics have been changed to protect the privacy of those depicted. Dialogue has been re-created from memory.

For E & H.

It's not what you look at that matters, it's what you see.

All good things are wild, and free.

Go confidently in the direction of your dreams.
Live the life you have imagined.

In wildness is the preservation of the world.

A man is rich in proportion to the number of things he can afford
to let alone.

If you have built castles in the air, your work need not be lost;
that is where they should be. Now put the foundations
under them.

— Henry David Thoreau

Contents

Contents

A Map of the Wild Year

Prologue

WE SAT, SIDE BY SIDE, in a wood-panelled room that smelled of polish and fear, wondering how we ended up here. Footsteps clattered on floorboards and threads of murmured conversations filtered through from adjoining rooms: voices of those who spent their days unravelling the messy tangles of other people's lives. E ran around us, playing games of imagination, singing made-up songs, blonde curls bobbing. Behind her were shelves lined with leaflets on divorce, custody and bereavement. In this cold and dismal room, she shone bright and golden, like a ray of sunshine breaking through clouds. Too bright, I thought. Too bright and too good for this place.

Without even needing to be seen by a judge, our petitions were granted and we were free to go. We left together, hand-in-hand, our children in our arms. I felt changed, somehow. Caught up within an almost overwhelming confusion of feelings:

sadness and failure and shame, but also a new glimmer of hope and possibility for the future. It wasn't the fresh start we had hoped and worked so hard for – for ourselves and our little family – but it was a fresh start of sorts. And it was done now, with no going back, becoming a part of our history that, for good or bad, would always be with us. Now, both in the wider context of our lives and, more immediately, our wild year, it was time to move on.

Beginning
At home in Wiltshire and the Peak District

IT WAS THE MEETING point of spring and summer, when the weather is always full of surprises. Only a few days earlier, we had watched as gales shook the blossom-heavy trees, covering the grass with petals like pink and white snow. And now it was hot, the wide Wiltshire sky stretching overhead, blue and empty save for the year's first swifts, wheeling, tumbling and screaming through the still air.

Out in the garden, grateful for a patch of shade, I leant against the trunk of the old apple tree, settling in to feed H, my newborn son. From this spot, through the tree's low-hanging boughs and across a lawn speckled with dandelions and daisies, I could see two-year-old E playing in a world of her own imagination. Barefoot on the soft grass, she was deeply fascinated by everything around her, touching, tasting, testing in order to really know the things she saw. Once, she told me, she had watched a bumblebee so close-up the breeze from its wings had tickled her skin.

She was three weeks into being a big sister. To our relief she had embraced this new role, quickly incorporating her baby brother's arrival into both her real and imaginary worlds. After H was born, Sim had taken two weeks' leave and we had closed the door on the outside world and drawn inwards, discovering, rediscovering ourselves as a family of four. I remembered how safe and secure I had felt then, relieved to be in the after lands of pregnancy and labour, my body so much easier to live in than it had been in those final, heavy weeks.

Already, though, that seemed like another time. With Sim now back at work, my days ebbed and flowed with the tides of love and fear, enthusiasm and exhaustion that is life with young children. The absolute, visceral attachment of mothering, and the state of existing where nothing gets done all day but the fulfilling of basic needs, had been a shock when E was born. This time around, I felt slightly more prepared for the way a new baby changes everything. Perhaps I was simply more accepting of the inevitable loss of control over even the smallest details of my days. I found – and still find – that each moment in my children's company feels like a completely new experience: a phenomenon that is both wonderful and terrifying.

But this gentle, all-consuming chaos was only half of our story – the half within which it was easy to live amid the busy brightness of our days. As the light faded each evening, my thoughts, too, grew darker, my sleepless nights filled with the impossible choices facing us. We had always aimed to live simply – to tread as lightly as we knew how. But even simplicity starts with sufficiency, and sufficient – when it came to money, at least, was something we no longer had.

*

H had not been the only new arrival in our lives that spring. Our first book had published the day before his birth. A real book – I could still barely believe it existed. That we had somehow turned this dream, which had on so many occasions during its creation felt beyond what was possible, into reality. A reality that was now sitting in bookshops across the country with our names on the cover.

The opportunity had come about by chance while on a walk with friends through the late summer Cotswold countryside. We had been sharing our passions for the great outdoors – theirs for wild swimming and ours for running, particularly off-road running, as a way of exploring and experiencing new places. Our friends are writers and photographers who had recently set up their own publishing company, creating beautiful guides to outdoor adventures. It all sounded incredibly exciting.

'Let us know if you ever decide to publish a running book!' I said as we exchanged goodbyes. A few days later, they emailed to ask if we were serious.

I showed Sim the email. 'Do you think we can write a book?'

'Of course we can!' he said, convinced, as always, that anything's possible if you throw everything into it.

We threw everything into it.

We bought a camera and learnt to take photos, working our way through how-to guides, going on courses and spending hours out on the hills shooting, editing, critiquing and trying again. We made regular trips around the country, researching new areas, finding new routes and taking thousands of photos.

Needing more time, space and money we moved from our rented house in the Cotswolds to the Peak District to live with Sim's parents so that we could work part-time while we wrote the book – me as a researcher and Sim as an on-call firefighter.

E was nearly one when we moved north; she loved living with her grandparents, who were in turn incredibly generous about sharing their house and lives with us. It also gave us the opportunity to experience running in the Peak District all year round. I learnt so much about running in the fells during this time, feeling my body growing stronger and faster with every passing month. We both loved running the local fell races, flying flat-out across the hills and the incredible friendliness of the finish line. We knew it would only be temporary, but it was a happy time for us all.

Before we had children, taking on big physical challenges was how we spent our free time. Back then, life had been all about triathlons, multi-day adventure races, mountain marathons and ultramarathons, the two of us supporting each other through the inevitable highs and lows of testing our mental and physical endurance. One of my favourite challenges was a coast-to-coast adventure race we did together, covering 100 miles of cycling, 10 miles of kayaking and 30 miles of running non-stop across Devon. During the final miles of the race, we found ourselves running through complete darkness – that inky blackness that only exists a long way from city lights – with our headtorches fading fast. My sleep-deprived brain was convinced we were going the wrong way, despite the fact that we were running along the South West Coast Path with the sea to our left, so rationally we couldn't be. After what felt more like days than hours we eventually, emotionally, spotted the lights of the finish on the headland ahead. Twenty-one hours after we had set out, we crossed the finish line, falling asleep as soon as we stepped into the van that would take us back to the start. We were the second team over the line that day and I was the only woman to finish, but the real win in my mind was the incredible adventure we had been through together. I was so proud of our strength as a team – working together, problem-solving, supporting and championing each other all the way, from start to finish. Writing our first book together drew on all of these strengths, and so much more.

After eighteen months in the Peak District, having worked our way through many crises of confidence, many late nights and early mornings, and our first experience of the intensity of the editing process, *Wild Running* was finished and ready for publication. It was time to move out of Sim's parents' house and find somewhere of our own again. By then, I was pregnant with H and longing for somewhere private – a space of my own to nest. We decided to return to the Cotswolds, where we had been living when E was born – a place that still felt more like home than anywhere else.

The little house we found to rent felt like the perfect place for our little family. It was on the edge of a village, high on a ridge between two deep, wooded river valleys – the Avon to the north and the Frome to the south – with views out across the Vale of Pewsey to the escarpment of Salisbury Plain beyond. Whichever way we explored took us straight into countryside. Out walking or running on our local trails, crossing fields, following rivers and winding through pockets of ancient woodland, we regularly saw herons, egrets, kingfishers, woodpeckers, roe and muntjac deer, barn owls and little owls, swifts, swallows and house martens, among many other creatures.

Out in the garden behind the house, Sim built a wooden playhouse for E, with a little slide attached; she helped, handing him nails. As the months passed, we let the neatly clipped grass grow wild, gently pointing out the bees and butterflies that now visited our garden to E. The once heavily pruned apple tree ecstatically reached its branches skywards, as if celebrating its newfound freedom. The roses rambled. Gravel migrated everywhere as the small stones became characters in E's games.

In May, H was born at home in our warm, sunny spare room.

*

Sitting beneath the apple tree on that hot afternoon, caught in a stiffening stillness by H's sleep, my mind turned to the almost constant worry of our finances. While, to an outsider looking in, life might look pretty much perfect, the truth was that we were running out of money. As each month passed it became more of a struggle to pay our rent and bills. Through the long nights, between feeds, I worried incessantly. I would lie still, smothered by darkness and uncertainty, searching for answers yet never finding them.

Our financial difficulties had begun soon after we moved into the house. After we left the Peak District, Sim had got a job working for a cycling charity, teaching kids to ride safely to school. But my fixed-term contract as a researcher had come to an end and, as my income over the past four years had been classed as a stipend, I also wasn't eligible for maternity pay. With a newborn baby and a toddler in my full-time care, I couldn't apply for regular jobs, and writing was bringing in barely anything. At first it wasn't a huge deficit, but it was enough that, as the weeks went by, our bank account steadily emptied and our debts increased.

There is a reason people talk of *feeling the pinch*. Not having enough money is an actual, physical feeling. It is always there – a cold grip of austerity, a constant reminder of being unable to afford the things – the life – that other people have. Like many of our generation, despite having degrees and jobs, we have both spent our adult lives in a state of just about managing. We had never minded too much, having passions like running which demanded little financial outlay, but now, with a young family to care for, it all felt very different, far more serious.

There are gaps in the complex weave of our society. Gaps where, unnoticed, people fall and are too often lost. When for one reason or another, their situation is out of the ordinary; when there isn't the correct box on a form; when people and their lives just don't fit. It might be gradual, or a sudden change in circumstances that switches a life from one that meets a certain set of criteria to one that does not. So it was with us.

We knew we were by no means the first family to find ourselves unable to meet our monthly outgoings – nor the last. Living in the modern world is expensive. When I left school and got my first job in the late 1990s, the average UK house price was £60,000. By 2021, this had risen to over £256,000. Wages, in real terms, have changed little, particularly for those in lower-income jobs. And renting doesn't offer an affordable alternative, difficult as ours is a generation of renters, spending, on average, a quarter of our pre-tax income on rent, up to half in some areas. So, when financial difficulties hit, we have no backup plan, no contingency fund, no Plan B.

I had looked in to whether we might be eligible for some kind of financial support, at least for a few months until I could find a new job, but our private landlord would not accept tenants on housing benefit. Moving back in with family was no longer an option – Sim's parents would soon be retiring, giving up the spacious house that had come with his dad's job as a vicar, and neither of my parents could accommodate a family of four.

Before long, our weekly shops started going on the credit card. I hated using it, but we often had no alternative as we waited for Sim's monthly wages or the infrequent payments for my writing commissions. The first thing I did when I woke up each morning was check our bank account. As the page loaded, I would feel my heart rate rising, a moment of nausea followed by crashing despair as the numbers appeared on the screen. On a couple of occasions, we had to borrow money from our families, overwhelmed with misery and shame as we steered our conversations towards the awful question. We were acutely aware that money was far from easy for them too but, when the alternative was being evicted, we didn't know what else to do.

As the weeks went by, both money and credit began to run out. Then the letters started to arrive: regular reminders that nothing we owned really *belonged* to us. Each one was less polite, more insistent, then threatening, all seemingly completely misunderstanding that we weren't doing this by choice. I couldn't imagine how we were going to get through this – what would happen when we simply could no longer afford to live? We had weathered lean times before. But now, with a family to care for and no obvious way out, we could feel that pinch tightening every day.

*

Sim took on more work, leaving early and finishing late, often missing out on every single one of the children's waking hours. He hated it, and the limitations that his absence placed upon us all. I continued to work freelance from home, writing whenever I had the chance but, with a new baby and a toddler in my care, the opportunities to do so were few and far between. No matter how hard we worked it was never quite enough: we always came up short. Not just on money but also on time. The time to be a family, the time to pursue the writing and photography work we dreamed might one day become our livelihood, the time to be ourselves.

During the week, while Sim was away at work, life was a blur of breastfeeding, nappy changing, love and guilt. I found myself descending into a place of private struggle. There was a growing darkness within my consciousness that I hadn't felt before; a creeping melancholy that lurked behind the need to be cheerful and efficient and practical.

I would often look at my children and feel the power and absoluteness of my love for them. I wanted more than anything to be the best possible mother – a shining example of warmth, enthusiasm, energy and inventiveness – but there were days, fogged by sleep deprivation and anxiety over our finances, when we barely managed to leave the house.

Until I met Sim I had never considered becoming a mother. I was never broody, never took any interest in other people's kids, to the point where some people reacted with open incredulity when I told them I was pregnant. But once Sim and I began to share our lives I found, to my surprise, that I could think of little else. Welcoming E, and then H, into our lives felt like the most natural, joyful thing possible. When E was born, I'd discovered I loved being a mother, surprising myself with these new skills of pregnancy and breastfeeding of which, after difficult starts on both counts, I found my body capable. It was a joy and a relief to discover motherhood came naturally when I had my own: I loved having babies and young children in my life, even though it was, at times, the hardest thing I had ever done.

During the long months of pregnancy before E had arrived, I had imagined that balancing motherhood with my other passions would be easy, or at least possible. Yet, as much as I found myself adapting to my new role, it was shock to discover that some of the worlds of which I had for so long been a part – that had for so long been a part of me – were no longer welcoming. There was the practical side of things – it is hard to fit babies into places and situations where there weren't any previously. But there was something else, too. Something less tangible. I didn't know if I had changed, or if others viewed me differently now that I had children. Perhaps it was a little of both. But I felt myself gradually changing in response; felt the hurt of the injustices entrenched in our daily lives more keenly by the day.

I was aware of an uprising, a surging, currently clouded by the daily fog of responsibility and sleep deprivation but growing in depth and strength, ready for a future time when I once again had a moment to myself to think, to process. I heard women in baby groups talking about the loneliness of being at home with full responsibility for one or more young children, but the only alternative was childcare and missing out on those precious years. I heard about something sociologists call the Motherhood Penalty, which places mothers behind both their childless peers and men in career and earning potential. Yet it didn't feel, to me, that it was motherhood that was the problem, rather the culture into which it had to fit. Where was the appreciation of the value of raising children well, both for their futures, and our own? Why did there seem to be so little value placed on parenting – the rearing of the next generation of humans, a generation that quite possibly might hold the fate of our species in their hands? I thought about their partners, like Sim, spending so much of their lives disconnected from family life. What of being involved, together, in this wonderful, vital and painfully brief facet of life? The flexibility that could allow parents to share working and caring for their children equally seemed cruelly absent for everyone involved.

Between navigating the needs of a baby and a toddler, I raged against these things we were simply supposed to accept. So many of the women whose work I admired – writers, artists, scientists, athletes – were childless: now I could see why. The simple act of mothering each day was challenge enough if done alone, without support, leaving little time for training, adventure or creativity. But by becoming mothers, women don't suddenly become less talented, less articulate, less passionate – they are simply silenced by inequality; by a lack of support; by a cultural, societal indifference.

Sim and I could both see so clearly that in sharing everything in our lives more equally, we could only be happier and more productive. Sharing parenting, work, daily chores and the freedom to escape to run along the trails or the towpath for an hour or so each day would mean we could all flourish and all support each other. I didn't want to have to separate and prioritise the things that were important to us; I wanted them all to be integral parts of one full, fulfilling, life.

There had to be a better way than this.

*

Finally, the school holidays arrived and Sim took two weeks off work. Money was now desperately tight but we were exhausted and strung out, in desperate need of an escape. So we packed our camping kit and headed back to the Peak District. As we inched our way along the M1, the kids sweaty and miserable in the back, I began wondering whether it might have been wiser to stay at home. Yet, despite the hours of singing, stories and snack stops, I couldn't wait to be back under canvas somewhere far from the daily struggles of work, finances and separation.

We camped at North Lees, a peaceful site run by the Peak District National Park Authority, a short walk across fields from the village of Hathersage. The moment we stepped out of the car we realised how much we had needed this escape. Having refused to nap for almost the entire journey, E and H were now fast asleep in their car seats. Making the most of us both having our hands free, we pitched the tent, made tea and, for the first time in what felt like months, sat down together and nobody cried.

Camping life was glorious. Early mornings were escapes from the warm, sleep-filled tent into the chill Derbyshire air. We took it in turns, running up to Stanage and along the tops of the gritstone edges, north to the Derwent Moors and Ladybower Reservoir; south along the edges of Burbage, Froggatt and Baslow. These were places we knew well from our time living nearby; it was good to be back. Running here, I felt more than a geographical remembering – it was as if my body also remembered, in its own sensory, proprioceptive way, how to run over these fells.

Absenting myself for an hour or so from mothering – a state so fully absorbed in itself it leaves little room for anything else – I thrilled in the peace and emptiness of these places on these runs. I could feel the movement – the diffusion – of anxiety and tension out of my body, and the essence of solitude in nature taking its place. Hard as it was to leave H when he was so tiny – when I could feel, viscerally, his terror at being parted from the person on whom he depended for everything – I knew I would be so much more able to be there for him, for all of them, when I returned.

After breakfast each morning, we followed E on her stop–start explorations of the camping field and surrounding woods, pointing things out, answering her constant stream of questions. We walked up to Stanage to marvel at the rock climbers or stayed near the tent reading to E or watching her play. Later in the day, while both kids napped in their slings, we walked together, discussing work and trying to find a way out of our financial problems. One afternoon, having driven across to Edale to explore somewhere new, we made it all the way up Jacob's Ladder to the Kinder plateau – the highest place in the Peak District – while the kids slept, lulled by the rhythm of our movement.

Those two weeks took us back to a life of sharing everything – caring for our children, daily chores, writing, long conversations about future projects and adventures, and tales from our solo runs. On our last evening I lay on my back in the tent, E and H on one side and Sim on the other, and tried to focus on the details; to soak in these precious moments that would all too soon be over. I felt, in a small way, that by living within this place we had become a part of it, and it a part of us: breathing the same air, synchronising to the same natural rhythms of light and dark, wakefulness and sleep.

As the last light of the day faded softly into darkness on the canvas overhead, instead of letting it soothe me to sleep as it had done for the past fortnight, I was wide awake, filled with dread about the long drive home the next morning, the looming return to normality. The worry and tension that had been blissfully absent during our stay started insidiously to creep back in, trickling through every part of my being.

I thought about the decisions we had made that had brought us to this point. Life had, not long ago, seemed so full of promise. We both had an education behind us, we had worked hard and we had made a considered decision to become parents. And yet here I found myself with no money, no job and no obvious way of doing anything about it until H was old enough to be looked after by someone else. And then what? Then I would spend my days working for other people, earning just enough to pay someone to look after my children, just enough to live in a house belonging to someone else. All I could see was a life that was, when it came down to it, barely our own at all.

Camping was a basic way to live, but there was such joy in its simplicity. And such freedom in it being all ours: our warmth, shelter and privacy, wherever we chose to pitch our tent. It was in that moment that I felt the first tinglings of a thought that made my heart race, my mind jump at the possibility of hope . . .

What if we didn't need to go back?

What if this way of life that had seemed to natural and so right over the past two weeks became our everyday? We could live, work and play together on far less money, on our own terms.

I thought of all the places we had glimpsed on our previous trips that we had so wanted to have the time to know better. I thought of the exhilaration and joy we had found in researching, writing and finally holding our very own book in our hands. We had little in terms of possessions or money, but we had plenty of camping kit. We regularly camped for two, three, even four weeks at a time. Would it really be so difficult, so different, to simply carry on?

Escaping

Life's shifting landscapes from London to wilder places

I HAVE ALWAYS BEEN DRAWN to the idea of escape. As a child I would escape to my treehouse – a few planks my dad had set high in a pear tree – from where I could watch and be with nature. Songbirds taught me the differences between their tunes; ants and woodlice invaded the old, damp wood; squirrels scampered past, not expecting a human to be sharing their tree, tails balancing as they leapt to the creosote-scented fence below. I loved reading about these creatures, learning their names in Latin, collecting wildlife magazines in ring-binders and using the photos to inspire my drawings. I was scientific in my approach, training my dad's unwieldy binoculars on nearby birds and butterflies or a magnifying glass on spiders in their silvery webs. Cradled in the comforting gnarled limbs of the tree, I could happily sit with my books and notepad for hours.

Back then, I remember feeling certain that I could live outside forever, fuelled by the nuts and berries I foraged from the garden and guided by books of survival and adventure. I was enchanted and inspired by the quests and magic and wild places in Tolkein's *Lord of the Rings*, Ursula K. Le Guin's *Earthsea* books and Susan Cooper's series, *The Dark is Rising*. I was also intrigued by the survivalist sense of freedom in John Seymour's books on self-sufficiency, which stood alluringly on my parents' bookshelves, and *Brendon Chase* by Denys Watkins-Pitchford, writing as the mysterious 'BB', about three boys who run away to live wild in the forest. These books felt like my life's backup plan, even then. It was all so real – so exciting – and such a long way from school.

I found school, and almost everything about it, a mystery. I was always in trouble. Stuck within the confines of the classroom, I would feel boredom and frustration boiling up inside me until I simply could no longer be still and quiet. Yet, by contrast, learning at home, surrounded by my parents' collection of reference books and their endless patience and creativity at finding me new things to do, felt fascinating and utterly involving. Primary school was confusing, lonely and often violent, the playground a concrete square surrounded by high wire fences. While the boys played football, I played sitting down games with the other girls while keeping an eye out for bullies. The only good thing about that school was riding home side-saddle on the crossbar of my dad's Raleigh, weaving through the London traffic, taking care to keep my feet out of his front wheel.

When I was ten, we moved from suburban north London to Herefordshire, my parents searching for a better place – a better way, perhaps – for my sister and I to grow up. It was such a big change. Suddenly, I was surrounded by the freedom of woods and fields. Whereas my outdoor world before had been limited mostly to our garden, now I had acres of wild space to roam, and I wanted to experience it all, to feel it beneath my feet, on my skin, in my hair. I'd stay out for hours, exploring with my beloved collie or riding bikes or horses. Home was a happy place, where I had both the love and the support I needed, and the freedom I wanted, but the secret of how to exist in the context of school continued to evade me.

I moved schools twice more, once on the strongly worded suggestion of the head teacher, finally ending up on a government-assisted place at a private school. The Assisted Places Scheme, established in 1981 to allow children from poorer backgrounds to attend independent schools, was abolished by Tony Blair's government in 1997, the year I left. Had it been a good idea? I certainly never felt like I fitted in, surrounded by children with wealthy parents while the state funded my fees, bus pass and uniform. And I still rebelled, endlessly rattling the bars of my perceived imprisonment. I thrilled in the feeling of simply walking away, missing lessons to spend afternoons exploring the banks of the River Wye or escaping to the local climbing wall to absorb and absolve myself in the joy of movement. I was often the only sixth-form pupil in detention, and always the only girl.

The year before my A levels, I fell ill with pneumonia and glandular fever. That same year, my parents split up and my dad, to whom I had always been close, moved out of our family home, taking my beloved collie with him. A month later, I fell off a friend's horse and fractured my pelvis, spending weeks on crutches and strong painkillers. Looking back now it is hardly surprising my exams didn't go well, but at the time I was convinced my failings were all my own.

It's a hard time to look back on now. I remember feeling as if the foundations on which I had built my life to that point – that had given me a grounded sense of who I was and where I wanted to go – were no longer there. I felt cast adrift, baseless, directionless. So I escaped, as soon as I could walk again, staying with friends in the Lake District, spending the summer discovering the power of being in higher, wilder places as a means of finding peace and calm amid the uncertainty.

A year later, having scraped through most of my A levels but having no idea what to do next, I decided to go further, plotting to cycle around Ireland. These were the days before the internet. There would be no blog detailing the minutiae of my daily travels, no beautiful Instagram gallery depicting a selection of carefully chosen moments, and no one anxiously awaiting my next update. I didn't even have a mobile phone.

I knew I would need to earn every penny I could before going, and that the cheaper my trip was, the longer it could be. I got a job in a call centre working mind-numbing, twelve-hour shifts. There were rivers, forests and mountains beyond the mirrored windows of the open-plan office, yet they reflected only the resignation of those inside. Working there strengthened my resolve to run away, and I spent my time dreaming about green hills and rugged coastlines, nights under the stars and pints of Guinness with strangers. Finally, I saved up enough to buy my kit: bike, tent, sleeping bag, panniers – the list gradually grew until I no longer knew how I'd fit it all on and still pedal.

On a rainy early summer's day, I caught a train across Wales to the sea at Fishguard, standing beside my heavily laden bike as the carriages swayed, struggling at times to keep it upright. On the ferry, I had to leave the bike below deck with the cars, chained upright in a hold that stank of fish and petrol. As the only cyclist, I was allowed off the boat first. I'll never forget that feeling as the ferry's front ramp slowly lowered, revealing the port at Rosslare and a grey ribbon of tarmac curving away into the distance. It was as if it was extending an invitiation: 'Go on, it's all yours to explore.'

That trip was everything I'd hoped – with some bits I'd prefer to have missed out. Cycling through the mountains, the incredible friendliness and passion for cycling that I experienced everywhere in Ireland, freewheeling along empty coastal roads while dolphins played in the waves below, crawling into my tent after a night of free drinks and folk music to find whichever way round I lay felt upside down. These were the highs I will never forget. But there was a dark side, too. While a desire for self-sufficiency and physical challenge were the main reasons I had set out – and the reason behind so many escapes since – that trip brought with it a level of stress and anxiety that I had never experienced before. And a frighteningly steep learning curve when it came to bike maintenance and cycling on busy roads with so much kit. At first, unused to clip-in pedals and with such a top-heavy bike, I'd simply fall over every time I had to stop.

And then there was the rain – I shouldn't have been surprised as the Emerald Isle is famous for it – days of being drenched and cold with nowhere to warm up or dry out. Eventually, I ran out of money four days before my ferry back to England, pedalling 100 miles on a single banana-flavoured energy gel. That trip taught me so much – about planning, self-reliance and the importance of not listening too much to the voices of doubt – both my own and others'.

*

Years later, lying there in the tent in the darkness of a Peak District night with Sim and our children asleep beside me, I thought again about everything that had brought us here. I thought about those times in the past when I had stepped away from the expected course of things, and the joy and fulfilment I had so often found in doing so.

'Sim, are you awake?'

He rolled over, placed a warm hand on my arm.

'What is it?'

'I've been thinking . . . What if we could live like this for longer? Give up the house and live in a tent. We could do it for a year – to start with, at least – like a challenge as well as a way out. We'd spend so much less and we'd all be together. What do you think? . . .'

*

After returning from Ireland, I had found myself lost all over again.

I lived in bedsits and shared houses for a few years, working temping jobs, making poor relationship decisions and scraping by. I worked in call centres, jobs selling timeshare holidays, mobile phone shops, supermarket checkouts, a factory packing frozen pastry, countless office admin jobs and even, for a brief spell, as a cleaner at Woolworths, where I buffed the wooden floors to a sickly smelling shine. I served coffee on trains and pulled pints in pubs, each for as long as I could bear. Then, at twenty-four, I married a man I'd known since school. Looking back, while I definitely wasn't ready to get married, I was ready to escape the life I'd been living.

A better decision was to start running every day, that and rock climbing regularly. Relishing the feeling of my body growing fitter and stronger, I met new people and explored new places. I also decided to go back to education, this time on my own terms. I booked evening classes studying A levels in chemistry and biology – subjects I'd been told I wasn't capable of at school – and then, with a NHS grant, student loan and several part-time jobs, I worked my way through a degree and then a master's in sport and exercise medicine.

At university, I discovered a passion for learning I had never experienced cooped up at school. I learnt to solve complex equations, use medical terminology and to treat each patient as if they were most important person I would see that day. I learnt to work really hard, and how it feels to give something everything you have. And for the first time in a long time, I had fun, experiencing real enjoyment and real fulfilment. I met many incredible people, some of whom have become precious, lifelong friends. It was the dawning of the realisation that I didn't need to accept what I was told I should or could do. That I'd never know what I was capable of unless I tried. *Really* tried.

By the time I was thirty, it was becoming obvious to both me and my then-husband that the relationship we were in was not built to last. We had changed so much since we first met, and that process had taken us in very different directions. There were no big arguments – no drama at all, really – just a gradual realisation that we no longer wanted to share our lives with each other.

That the marriage was over finally became clear as I lay on a hospital bed in the major injuries unit at the Royal Devon and Exeter Hospital. I was in the final few weeks of training for the UK Ironman triathlon – a 2.4-mile swim, 112-mile cycle and 26.2-mile run – and had fallen off my bike on a fast A-road, halfway through a 6-hour training ride. The driver in the car behind me, who was thankfully paying attention, watched as I cartwheeled through the air and landed on my head. He rang 999 and a helicopter came and collected me, flying me back to where I'd set out on my bike three hours earlier in less than fifteen minutes.

After several X-rays and numerous other tests, I was given the all-clear, escaping with a headache, plenty of cuts and bruises and a scar on my chin that will be with me for the rest of my life. But the hardest-hitting moment of the day was not the 40-mph impact with the road. It was seeing the man I was married to walking into the hospital looking not concerned, but bloody irritated.

As soon as I could walk again, I moved out of the flat we had shared for five years and into a house-share in a beautiful Devon longhouse. But this, too was a strange time, co-existing yet never really connecting with the people I lived with. I threw myself into sport, spending every weekend racing or going out on self-devised epics so I never had too much time to think. There were days when I would leave at dawn and cycle Devon's lanes to Dartmoor, battling the hills and gales until I could turn around and arrive home by dusk. I was working in a sports injury clinic during the week, cycling to and from work and seeing patients each day, thrilling in this newfound independence. I loved it, but it was hard and I was often wrecked with tiredness. After one particularly long day, I fell asleep on my ride home.

A few weeks later, I finished the Ironman, swimming breaststroke as the crash had left me unable to lift my right arm above my head. Crossing the finish line after a day of swimming, cycling and running around Lancashire, a wave of emotion unlike anything I'd felt before hit me, bringing me to my knees. It made the hairs on the back of my neck prickle, my chest tighten and my eyes fill with tears. My brilliantly supportive sister had travelled to Bolton with me but she was back at the start; there was no one I knew at the finish, so I quietly sobbed to myself as emotion overflowed. Crossing that line felt like the culmination of a whole series of much longer and much more complicated challenges than finishing a long-distance triathlon.

It was Sim, when we had only just started seeing each other, who encouraged me to give the Ironman a go when everyone else, including me, thought I should probably pull out. We had met years before when were both working part-time in a climbing shop, partly to fund our university studies, partly to take advantage of the generous discounts on outdoor kit. He was good-looking, confident, socially at ease and younger than me – all the things I usually managed to avoid in a partner. What struck me most, though, was his seemingly inexhaustible enthusiasm. He would bound up to customers that the rest of us were studiously ignoring, and his knowledge of outdoor kit was encyclopaedic.

I had no idea, when I first met him, wielding a vacuum cleaner with a surprising level of expertise for someone of twenty and even looking like he was enjoying it, that Sim and I would one day join our lives together; that his enthusiasm and energy would become such an important part of my every day. I had thought, back then, that we were very different. But, as it turned out, we share many of the same passions and the same attitude to life. We both grew up with parents working unusual hours in creative professions rather than nine-to-five in an office. Neither of us had had a TV, instead spending our time climbing trees and running around outside. In our own ways, we had often felt different from those around us – although where Sim has the rare ability to fit in everywhere, I usually felt I fitted in nowhere. We both have a strongly developed self-reliance, which only truly found a place in our adult lives when we were living outside normality, outside the zones of comfort and convenience.

Meeting Sim felt like coming home after many years adrift. Right from the start, our relationship worked in every way, and it remains one of the very few things in life I have never questioned. He understood and accepted me without any demands to change, to be different, to be more like someone else – from my love of being outdoors and of pushing myself to my limits, to those times when I need to withdraw from the world into a quiet place or remove myself from a situation that isn't working for me. We are our own people but we make a great team.

Two months after we started going out, we moved in together. Two years later, when I was six-months pregnant with E, we got married. We had a tiny ceremony surrounded by our closest family and friends, and did everything for the wedding ourselves, from cooking and cleaning to decorating. Everything, that is, other than our two beautiful wedding cakes. Sim's mum made one of her legendary fruitcakes, decorated with our entwined initials and heart-shaped sweets, and my dear friend, Sarah, made the other – the lightest, most perfect Victoria sponge. Sim's dad conducted the ceremony and the local bellringers rescheduled that week's practice to serenade us for free.

We spent our wedding night camping under a beautiful old hornbeam tree, and then packed our rucksacks and headed for Cornwall for a fortnight walking the coastal cliffs and peaceful beaches, sleeping in our backpacking tent, making the most of those last few weeks of being just the two of us.

*

From the moment we made our decision to go camping for a year, everything felt different. Suddenly there was the possibility of an end to our financial struggles in sight, and a big adventure to look forward to. Time together became time for planning; time apart was a reminder that things would soon be different. During the long, wakeful nights now I could think about camping and exploring together. For the first time in a long time I felt that building excitement of an adventure on the horizon.

Was I simply running away again? And, if I was, was that really such a bad thing? Under some circumstances perhaps it's actually the best thing to do – embracing exploration of the unknown, both within and outside ourselves, over routine and safety. It can be a powerful way to take back control of a life that seems to be happening despite our wishes and preferences, rather than because of our choices. Every time I have chosen to flee – from school, jobs, relationships and situations – it has been an act of survival, removing myself from something that, deep down, I knew was no good for me. But this time I wasn't alone. We were escaping together, as a family, when we realised that the life we wanted – both for our children and ourselves – was not the one we were living.

Perhaps strangely, I felt neither fear nor trepidation. I don't think either of us wondered whether it was the right decision. We recognised there would be lows and highs and that we needed to work out the finer details of the year, but we thought it could work, if we gave it everything. As the saying goes, sometimes you have to jump off the cliff first and build your wings on the way down.

We started planning straight away, working out when Sim would need to hand in his notice, when we would give up the house and what we would need to buy or borrow to make it all possible. Sim's parents had recently bought a tiny, remote cottage on the edge of Dartmoor for their retirement but wouldn't be moving in until November. They generously offered it to us as a place to stay for the month of October. We jumped at their offer – it was an incredible stroke of good fortune and gave us a starting point: precious time between leaving behind the busy stresses of our old life and moving into the tent to begin our new one. As we would pretty much have to camp in the cottage

– there was no furniture, carpets or curtains – we hoped it would make our transition into the wild a little gentler.

Having the cottage for October also meant our year of camping would, necessarily, begin in November. How would we fare going straight into the cold, dark months, our kit untested, at the mercy of the weather? It was something we would need to plan for carefully, but really there wasn't anything else we could do. We would need to deal with winter at some point – at least this way we could get it over and done with and have the warmer, drier weather to look forward to.

Late one evening, once the kids were asleep, we sat down together and worked out a budget. We factored in the income we knew we'd have – our monthly child benefit payment and weekly tax credits – and our estimated income from freelance work and the royalties from our book, which we hoped would start to arrive that autumn. We needed to more than halve our monthly rent from the £800 we had been paying for the house to around £10 per night for camping. This was likely to be higher over the summer, but we were aiming, by negotiating deals on longer-term camping pitches and offering our services as labour or house-sitters, that it would average out over the year. Some bills, like council tax, would be taken out of our budget altogether. Others, including fuel for heating and cooking would be reduced. And then there were the inevitable outlays we couldn't predict, including those for a vehicle.

One big worry was our credit card and loan debts, which had continued to mount up over the preceding months. We had paid off what we could, but we also needed money to live on. As each statement arrived, I looked with horror at the amount of interest we were being charged – it was about the same as our monthly payments. I scrolled through debt advice websites, which suggested switching to interest-free alternatives, but our increasingly fragile credit rating and lack of income ruled this out. We wanted to avoid defaulting on these debts if at all possible, so, depressing as it was that we were barely paying anything off the overall totals, we added the minimum payments to our budget. We were doing everything we could to put ourselves into a better position to clear them one day.

A positive, at least, was that over many years of adventures, both separately and together, we had accumulated a lot of camping kit. Our main expense would be a tent large enough for the four of us to live in comfortably for a year or more. Our trusty Hilleberg backpacking tent, which had seen us through many adventures before, was perfect for shorter trips, and we had total faith in its ability to withstand anything the Great British weather could throw at it, but it gave us very little space aside from sleeping. The final decisions on kit would wait until we moved to Dartmoor, when we would have the time to research more thoroughly. But, looking at the sums as they stood, the tent and everything else we needed before we set out could cost no more than £1,000.

One of the first things we needed to do was swap our sensible family car for a vehicle that would see us through a year of living wild. It needed to be reliable, safe, capable of off-roading even during the winter months and have lots of storage space. And all for the same value as our current car so we could do a straight exchange. We read and researched and perused the second-hand car sales ads, eventually finding one that sounded perfect. It was a red pickup truck – a Mitsubishi L200 – ageing but with fairly low mileage and from a garage that would offer an exchange for our old car. We went to view it straight away. The first time we all climbed in and took it out for a test drive we knew instantly it was perfect. Sitting in the cab, high above the road, it already felt like we were on an adventure.

We also began thinking about where our wild year would take us. There were places we needed to visit for work – commissions for magazines and content for the future books we wanted to write – and places we wanted to visit to learn about and immerse ourselves in. Our loose plan was to spend the winter in Devon and Cornwall, making the most of the milder climate and enjoying the beaches and moors in the absence of the summer tourists. And then, once spring arrived, we would head north.

As August drew to a close, with a month to go, we gave our notice on our house and advertised our possessions on second-hand websites. Sim also handed his notice in at work and that would take us almost to the end of September. There was a lot to do but with E and H to look after and articles to write at the weekends, I had little chance of getting much done before then. At best we would have a couple of days to pack and attempt to restore the house and garden to something resembling how it had been when we first moved in.

It was strange yet oddly exhilarating to watch the house emptying, as strangers came into our home and dismantled it, piece by piece. There was a thrill in the letting go, and in the knowledge that we would soon have no need for all these *things* that had been part of the life we were leaving behind. We were choosing freedom, with all its uncertainties, over a familiarity and security that we knew would never bring us joy.

The only thing we couldn't sell or give away were our books, of which we had many, collected separately and then together over the years. We packed them up in boxes, ready to store at Sim's parents' house for the year, along with a few things that we might need for our future life, whatever that might look like. Finally, a young couple arrived to take the dining table and chairs that stood alone in the middle of the otherwise empty living room. They were standing on the doorstep holding hands when I went to let them in. Moving in together for the first time – filled with excitement, hopes and dreams for the future – they reminded us a little of how we had been, just a few years earlier, when responsibilities weighed less heavily and it hadn't seemed to matter so much that we only saw each other at weekends. Back then, it had been different: there were fewer of us to share this time between. Perhaps, too, we hadn't thought to really think about it; hadn't yet considered there might be any other way. But now we, too, were starting our own next chapter.

On that final night after the table had disappeared through the door, we sat together on the floor in the middle of an empty space that had been our home. We had lived in this house for less than a year but it had, for that short time, felt like a real, grown-up home. It had been warm, comfortable and . . . almost frighteningly normal. It had offered that safe space I had so craved during the later months of pregnancy. But now it had served that purpose. Even without our financial problems, I'd known this house was never a long-term option for us – it was too warm, too comfortable and definitely too expensive. We craved the exhilaration of a wilder kind of life, along with the freedom to make choices about how and with whom we spent our days. We wanted to fully experience the rawness and the realness of living by our own means. To throw ourselves into the world, rather than simply watching it pass us by.

AUTUMN

'Life starts all over again when it gets crisp in the fall.'
F. Scott Fitzgerald, *The Great Gatsby*.

Halfway House
A cottage on Dartmoor

THE FIRST SIGNS OF autumn were just beginning to emerge as we made our final preparations to leave. Early morning mists gathered in the valleys, hedgerows held the last of the summer blackberries and leaves on the layered patchwork of the woods hinted at the golds and russets to come. On our last morning at the house, E, who had recently turned three, ran out onto the dewy grass, gasping wide-eyed at its coldness on her warm, bare feet.

The house was empty now. It sounded different as I walked between the rooms, finding echoes where I wasn't expecting them. The few possessions we would need when we moved back into a house at some currently unimaginable point in the future – our big mattress, boxes of books, kitchen equipment, E's climbing frame and the potted Christmas tree we had bought for E's first Christmas – had all been found temporary homes with various family members.

As Sim tessellated the last of our kit into the truck, I went out to find E, who was playing with her stones in the garden. I looked around at the little square of grass and its edging of earthy beds, scraggly and sombre now the flowers had finished. We had managed to return the place to a slightly rewilded version of its former neatness, but we couldn't bring ourselves to prune back the old apple tree. I hoped it was enough – we needed our deposit back.

'We're saying goodbye to the house today,' I said gently to E. We had talked about the trip, and she had always seemed enthusiastic about the idea, but I wasn't sure how she would feel when it came to the actual moment of leaving.

'I know,' she said, her intense blue gaze meeting mine. 'We're going to live in a tent!' Her smile was joyful, excited, completely free of worry. She was simply ready to get on with the adventure. I picked her up and gave her a big hug, more grateful than she could possibly have known for her cheerful optimism.

Stepping through the door for the final time, I laid a hand against the wall of the house, pausing for a moment. I had no doubts about what we were doing and, in almost every way, we were taking everything important with us. But in the heart of the house that sunny room where H had been born was a place we would almost certainly never see again. So full of meaning and relevance to us it would, to the new inhabitants of the house, simply be a spare bedroom with pretty yellow curtains. I felt a small part of us would always remain here though, felt a tug at my heart for the harshly temporary nature of renting. A reminder of the gulf between those who own properties and those who don't.

It would be a place I would think of often, feeling the call to return one day to this wooded stretch of the Avon valley where we had begun our family life together and welcomed our children. We had also become good friends with the family opposite, who had children the same ages as our own. E and their daughter had played together over the past months, and I felt a niggle of guilt at taking her away from her friend. We would all miss them of course, but this friendship, I knew, would be something we took with us.

I looked over to where Sim and the kids were waiting for me in the truck. It was time to go. Closing the door, I dropped the keys through the letterbox and joined them.

*

It should have been a two-hour drive to the cottage but, in the way of things with babies and small children, it took us nearly five. Eventually, we made it to the estate agent in the town of Bovey Tracy to pick up the keys to the cottage. I looked up at Dartmoor, rising above the houses, its lower slopes green with woodland, the higher hills bare and golden in the afternoon sun. I tried to hold onto the feeling of experiencing this place for the first time, before it all became familiar and every day. To notice and record how somewhere looks, feels, smells when it is previously unknown, when we can see it more clearly and essentially than we ever do again, when we continue to look but cease to be able to really see. That was something I wanted to do consciously in every place we visited over the coming year – to capture that very first experience and its subsequent mellowing and softening with time. To experience every place both as strange and, later, as familiar.

In town, we stocked up on food – although the cottage currently had no furniture, we were relieved to learn that it did have a fridge and cooker, left by its previous inhabitants. We wedged the shopping into the small remaining gaps in the truck, the rest on my lap, then drove the final miles, climbing steadily up and over the moor, gorse and bracken-cloaked hills rising steeply to one side and falling away to the other. From the narrow road, we gazed down onto the tops of the trees in the valley far below. Beyond that, fields and towns and then, just visible on the horizon, the shifting glimmer of the sea.

Dropping off the open moor along the course of a river, we followed lanes lined with old stone walls, barely wide enough for the truck to pass through. Everything was covered in a dense patchwork of green: every tree, wall, boulder and stretch of ground had its own party of mosses, lichens, fungi and ferns. We looked at each other, impressed, though not surprised, that Sim's parents had chosen somewhere so wildly adventurous to spend their retirement.

Having only seen the cottage in photos and imagined over the passing weeks how it might feel to finally be there, it was exciting to be discovering and experiencing it all for the first time. We left the truck packed and went exploring, E running ahead and H gazing up at the moving, dappling light and shade from his perch on my hip . We toured the little granite house with its two rooms downstairs and three up, and the space outside – woodland, tracks, fields dotted with granite boulders and the moor above – as E's excited words carried through the quiet air. I felt a wave of gratitude for having everything we needed right here with us. For the freedom of so few ties. And for having the cottage for this important month of planning.

Returning to the truck, we unpacked everything into the two downstairs rooms, arranging a raft of camping mats on the floor, held together with mattress protectors and sheets. It would do for now, but we would need to work out something more permanent for our sleeping arrangements. After a makeshift supper, we sat out in the little yard at the back, watching the sun slip below the hills, plunging the valley into cool shadow that made us shiver. Then we retreated to the cottage and slept on the floor, windows wide open, surrounded by the night-time sounds of the moor.

*

Waking early on our first morning on Dartmoor, I lay quietly for a while in the warm space beneath our big, shared duvet, enjoying the gentle mingling of breath and bodies. Through the curtainless window I could just see the first bluing of the still-dark sky, etched with the silhouettes of gently waving branches overhead. H began to stir, his tiny hands reaching for me though his eyes were still closed. I gave him his first feed of the day, lying still beside him until I was sure he had fallen back into deep sleep. I was thankful to my body for being able to feed him, an instant source of comfort as well as everything he needed to grow healthily until he was six months old. It was a relief to know that we wouldn't need to deal with sterilising bottles and sourcing formula in the tent – and there was another benefit, too. With both children, breastfeeding gave me two years free from menstruation. I had managed periods while camping on many occasions previously, but it was liberating to know I would probably not need to deal with them alongside everything else this year.

I was impatient to go exploring, to begin the process of getting to know this part of the moor. Inching free from H's grasp, desperate not to wake him up as I did so, I slipped out of bed and pulled on my running kit. Leaving both children snuggled up with Sim, I let myself silently out into the cool freshness of the moorland morning, the damp air heavy with the musty scents of autumn.

Outside, the world was alive with sound: the shrill chatter of birds, the rush and babble of the nearby brook, the whisper of the wind through drying autumn leaves. It was a feeling of total immersion, of richness and density, of sensual overload that demanded only that I gave myself up to it, became a part of it.

For the first few minutes I walked, allowing body and world to reach a point of equilibrium, feeling the movement and resulting warmth easing the stiffness of the night. Then, slowly at first, I started to run, discovering tracks that led away in every direction: straight up through fields towards the tors on the horizon; winding on bright green grassy walks through birch and beech and oak; or out on the long curve of the driveway, the remnants of a once-grand estate entrance. That morning, high with excitement, I headed straight for the top of the moor, embracing the challenge of body against gradient, refusing to let myself slow before I'd reached my goal.

Running has always been a part of life for me – another way to escape, perhaps – but also a means of exploring and of immersing myself in each place I live or visit. It is a source of ideas and inspiration, time and space to work things out and sometimes simply a way to achieve oblivion through physical effort. Running has been there on many occasions when I have doubted and struggled with myself and those around me, its rhythm bringing order and comfort to my whirling thoughts, transporting me to a place where I feel like the truest version of myself. While I am almost ashamed to admit it, I know I will be an easier person to live with – kinder to both myself and those around me – if I have started the day with a run.

Laying a hand on the cold, hard stone of the summit cairn, I finally allowed myself to stop, legs burning with effort and lungs desperately sucking in the cold morning air. I spun slowly on the spot, taking in the vast view all around me. A long ridge ran away to the south, claiming rocky tors as it skirted the edge of a deep valley, ending at the distinctive rounded bulk of Haytor. These tors are the bare knuckles of a vast, granite pluton – a layer of underground rock that bubbled into being some 280 million years ago – exposed by millennia of weathering and erosion. To the north the moor seemed endless, falling away into a deep valley and then rising to a high point far away on the horizon. To the east, I could see again the silver-blue glint of the sea.

It was so quiet. Like a great blanket of silence almost deafening in its absence of sound. At first it felt almost uncomfortable as my ears strained and rang with the unaccustomed stillness. But gradually, I became aware of the more subtle tones – the babble of a skylark, my own breath – easing now after the climb – the gravel crunch of decomposing granite underfoot, the rhythmic smack of an axe on wood in the dense tangle of trees far below.

I felt myself begin to relax into the peace of it all, able now to notice, and appreciate, the intricate layering of sounds that had been for so long drowned out by a background roar I hadn't even realised was there. I thought of the stresses we had left behind – the rush of mornings as Sim left for work, the drawing-out of the days that were at once so solitary and yet so full of needs, the weight of financial worry – and revelled in the lightness of their absence.

Up on that high part of the moor, as the initial spike of exhilaration begin to recede, as being and landscape softened into easier companionship, I could feel my body cooling, the chill October air creeping beneath my clothes. I felt cleansed and restored right through by the exertion, the push of the breeze, the peacefulness and aloneness of this place, and utterly ready to return to the life that awaited me back at the cottage. I launched myself from the top, running fast all the way back, flying down the rough track with pure joy and abandon of the kind I remembered from childhood. Reaching the sheltered stillness of the valley, I made my way to the edge of the brook and splashed the cold, clear water over my face and hair. I felt feral and alive, infused with the energy of the wild.

Back in the empty kitchen, I told Sim about my run as we made coffee on the gas hob. I scooped up H, who, sensing my return and his imminent second breakfast, was just waking up in the big makeshift bed in the room next door. We took our coffee out to join E, who had already found a new family of stones in the little yard at the back of the house. She was lining them up, her head tilting to get a better view, the morning sun in her hair, already back in that imaginary world that she carried everywhere with her.

We had packed up one life but we were still a long way from being ready for our new one. We still had no tent, no heat, light or anything more permanent than camping mats to sleep on. We would need to book all our pitches for the winter months before we left, knowing campsites in the UK that open year-round were few and far between. We hoped that later in the year we would be able to book late or simply turn up, giving us the flexibility to travel to different locations for work and whim.

We soon discovered there was no mobile signal anywhere near the cottage, so I spent an hour standing up on the moor, battling with the wind, trying to arrange for the internet to be connected. The following days, as we waited for the router to arrive, were a reminder of how dependent we had become on this instant, constant connection. In some ways, this brief period of disconnection allowed us to experience our peaceful position even more deeply; in others it added extra stress that we might be missing opportunities for work. Eventually the package arrived. It was a relief to plug everything in and find it worked, linking – if very slowly – our remote hideaway with the rest of the world.

Our first job was to find a tent for the four of us to live in. It had to be large enough to give us the space we would need for such a long trip, yet small enough to fit within a standard tent pitch; tough enough to withstand wind and rain and being put up and down hundreds of times over the next year or more, yet with a pack-size small enough to fit in the back of the truck with everything else. It also needed to be able to house a stove for cooking and warmth.

We eventually settled on a 6-metre Emperor Ultimate bell tent, with two heavy-duty main poles and plenty of room inside for the four of us, all our kit and a woodburning stove. It was a vast, cotton canvas mansion, nearly 3 metres high, but it would fit into the back of the pickup and still leave just about enough space for the rest of our kit. Better still, it was an ex-demo model and half price. We arranged to pick it up in time for our November start, from a warehouse on the outskirts of Guildford.

For warmth and cooking we chose a Frontier stove: compact, robust and simple, and suitable for use both inside – the flue passing through a hole in the tent roof to take smoke away from our living quarters – and outside the tent, over the summer months. These stoves were originally designed for humanitarian aid use, which would mean it should be easy to maintain and fix should anything go wrong. The legs and flue packed neatly inside the main unit, making it ideal for our limited space. We bought a metal water tank, which wrapped around the flue and rested on a corner of the stove to boil water quickly and efficiently while taking up minimal stove-top space.

Camping with a woodburner and two small children, we couldn't afford any risk of a fire. We bought a spark arrestor – a cylinder of wire mesh that fitted over the top of the flue – a fire blanket and an extinguisher. We also bought a pocketknife each, useful for many tasks throughout the day, but also a means of cutting through the canvas to escape in an emergency.

I had H asleep in his sling on my front when we went to choose my knife from a tall glass cabinet in an outdoor shop.

The sales assistant looked at me dubiously as I fumbled with opening each knife at arms' length, not wanting to hold them above my sleeping baby. Eventually, I decided on a slim, single-blade model with a curved wooden handle that fitted snugly into my hand. I would grow to enjoy having in my pocket, appreciating its keenness for everything from sharpening E's colouring pencils to opening packets of food. And, if it came to the worst and I needed to cut my way out of the tent, I trusted it completely.

Our final purchase, using up the last of the budget we had allocated for kit, was two double roll-up, thickly padded cotton mattresses, which we had delivered to the cottage as we were already finding our camping mats uncomfortable. Getting the best possible sleep would be essential to staying healthy and happy over the coming year, and we didn't want to spend night after night on inflatable camping mats with the ever-present possibility of a puncture. These new mattresses would be far warmer to sleep on and as close to a normal bed as possible when made up with sheets and duvets.

Throughout this time we had spent hours exchanging emails with campsite owners, farmers and friends-of-friends, arranging places to pitch our tent. Some of our stays would be free in return for work – writing, photography or looking after a house or garden while the owners were away – while others were simply happy to offer us a generous discount over the winter months.

We had decided that over the course of the coming year we wanted to give ourselves the time to really get to know Britain's wilder places – its National Parks, Areas of Outstanding Natural Beauty, and hidden pockets of nature – by living within them.

We wanted to learn as much as we could about these places: the forces that shaped them and the life that thrived – or otherwise – within them.

Biodiversity loss, happening at a startling rate even within our own lifetimes, means our children are growing up surrounded by less nature than we did, a fact that tears at my heart. Many of the creatures I watched in my childhood garden, from hedgehogs to bullfinches, are now rarities. We wanted to understand the pleasures and plights of our wild flora and fauna better, wanted to help our children grow into adults for whom the natural world would be so important, so precious, that living in a way that accelerated its loss could simply not be an option.

The UK has fifteen National Parks – areas whose landscape, wildlife and cultural heritage have the highest levels of protection by law. This protection aims to 'conserve and enhance natural beauty, wildlife and cultural heritage', as well as promoting public understanding and enjoyment. A shock was discovering through further research that Britain's National Parks don't meet the internationally accepted standard for that designation. Unlike those in the US, which include Yellowstone and Yosemite, here in the UK, people live, work and farm in our National Parks. Activities like hunting and extraction are allowed and much of the land is privately owned.

Areas of Outstanding Natural Beauty, of which there are currently forty-six in the UK, have a similar level of protection. Sim and I had lived in the Peak District and several AONBs between us. We had also both spent plenty of time on Dartmoor, but most of our previous visits to the UK's protected landscapes had been limited to a week or two at a time. It was an exciting prospect to really experience and get to know them from within. From the ground – on which we would spend our nights – up.

Gradually, our plans began to fall into place. After collecting our tent, we would spend the first month in the south-east, exploring the New Forest and South Downs, the UK's most recently designated National Parks. Then we would work our way westwards, dividing our time between the National Parks of Dartmoor and Exmoor and their numerous neighbouring AONBs. Once spring arrived, bringing with it warmer, more settled weather, we would start heading north, taking in the Peak District – the UK's first National Park – the Yorkshire Dales and the Lake District. After that, we would see what time we had left and where work would take us.

Counterflow

Immersion in Dartmoor life

As OCTOBER GOT UNDERWAY, life in the cottage quickly settled into a natural routine, guided by the rhythms of light and dark, the wants and needs of our children and the demands of our work. Our new striped mattresses arrived and we slept on them in the main downstairs room, deciding it was easiest just to keep one room warm. On colder mornings, we lit the little open fire, taking it in turns to spend a few hours working, one of us using a storage box as a makeshift table for our laptop, the other playing or reading with the children. When the skies were clear we watched as the sun rose over the surrounding moor, flooding it with luminous red, then gold, then bright sparkling light that made the colours sing.

E didn't seem to notice the lack of furniture, having been happy to sit and play on the floor even when we'd had chairs. Out in the woods near the house, she ran ahead as we walked, weaving between the trees, scrambling over fallen logs and up onto big granite boulders, splashing with excited shrieks in the cold, shingly shallows of the brook. One particular boulder, higher up on the moor and set next to a hawthorn tree, gnarled and twisted by the moorland weather, was her favourite, commanding far-reaching views to both Haytor and Hound Tor. She loved to sit at the very top, surveying the landscape which stretched out all around her. This place became known to us as E's Island.

In the afternoons, we explored further afield, following rough tracks through ancient oak woodland where stunted trees grew gnarled and twisted, hairy with moss, lichen hanging from their boughs like wizards' beards.

Parts of Dartmoor like this one are home to pockets of rare temperate rainforest, which would once have covered vast swathes of western Britain. In these places, hidden from development and destruction by humans, high rainfall and low temperature variation nurtures a moist, sheltered environment for wild things to flourish. There is an astounding amount of life in these places – every rock, trunk and branch growing its own forest of polypody ferns, lichens and mosses. Epiphytes – plants that grow upon others – thrive in a symbiotic soup of damp life. Beneath the human world of well-worn trails, ants and beetles follow their own ways and, deeper still, roots and fungal hyphae creep along underground networks. Here in these deeply alive, deeply green places, immersed in the textures, scents and sounds all about us, was the nurturing, interconnected, richly varied life we were hoping to find.

Ancient remnants of lives long past lie scattered across Dartmoor's 368 square miles, and there were some fascinating ruins within easy reach of the cottage. A short walk up an overgrown track brought us to the crumbling remains of a former farm, with the large farmhouse and barn standing roofless and entwined with a dense weave of ivy. Late one afternoon, as we approached, a tawny owl flew out from the rafters, swooping away into the woods. Inside the old house, the hearth that would once have been the roaring heart of the house, stood cold and quiet, set into a thick stone wall. Searching for more information about the farm, I found a single image of it as it had once been, in a grainy black-and-white photograph dated 1902.

Higher up on the moor we explored the ruined medieval village at Hound Tor, wandering the rectangular outlines of traditional Devon longhouses and imagining how it must once have smelled and sounded. These shared dwellings would once have sheltered animals at one end, a family at the other. Farmed since Neolithic times and, by the eleventh century, home to six households, *Hundatora*, as it was originally known, was deserted in the late fourteenth or early fifteenth century, probably due to weather, famine, plague, or all three. I found these lasting echoes of those who had gone before us strangely anchoring.

One afternoon, after a frantic morning working to meet a deadline, I left Sim with a sleeping E and H and walked slowly down to the brook. Rising high on the open moor above and flowing down the granite hillside through a channel carved by its own persistence, its music was a constant backdrop to life in the valley.

The afternoon was warm for October, the lush grass of the bank cool under my feet as I stepped out of my shoes and rolled my shorts up as high as they would go. I made my way down to the shingle beach, a place where we had seen signs of otters, and watched the busy water rushing past. The peat of the moor had stained it a clear brown, like fine black tea, my bare feet taking on the same hue as I stepped in. The water's icy coldness flooded through me, awakening and sharpening my senses. I waded further in then, turning upstream and bracing myself against the water's push, I started to walk. Each step felt new and alive with sensations as my feet sank into shingle, slipped on weed-covered rocks, stumbled with pain as sharp stones cut into my skin. In places the bed dropped away, the water rising to my thighs, making me gasp aloud with the shock of the cold. I noted a couple of deeper pools, far too deep for wading, to come back to and swim another time.

It was a strange journey, surging against the brook's ceaseless resistance. At times I found myself trapped on its course, hedged in by the giant hogweed and hemlock water dropwort, which reared threateningly to either side. This latter plant has the dubious accolade of being the UK's most poisonous plant, so I gave it and its irritant companion a wide berth as I walked.

After half-an-hour or so, I could stand the building pain in my feet no longer and took advantage of another shingle beach to escape the world of the brook. I wandered back to the cottage, skin drying in the sun, my mind bursting with words that I had to get down on paper. Some time later, 'Counterflow', the poem I wrote that day, and some of the photos of the brook taken during those weeks at the cottage, were, to my delight, accepted for publication in *Waymaking*, an anthology of women's outdoor art and writing.

Between childcare, exploring our local surroundings, writing, and researching kit, I read voraciously, trying to find stories of others who had embarked on similar journeys. It seemed there were very few. I found numerous tales of lone adventurers and intrepid teams, leaving everything behind and heading off on grand expeditions to remote and often dangerous places. I thought of those they left at home – families, partners, friends – keeping everything together as best they could, daily dreading a phone call that would bring bad news.

These were huge endurance challenges that required months, or even years, of commitment and vast sums of money. They were undertaken mostly by men, and definitely without babies. I had read and loved many of these books throughout my life, fascinated by the conquering of mountains and deserts, the history of exploration, and the physiology and psychology of survival in extreme environments. But they felt such a long way away from the adventure we were planning. Was it possible, I pondered, to make this trip as exciting and challenging as these feats of endurance I loved reading about, but to do it all together, as a family, bringing our young children along for the adventure with us? Could we do this starting with so little in the bank, just earning what we needed as we went? And would we be able to use the next year to build up our self-employed work so that, longer term, we could live in a happier and more fulfilling way than that we had recently left behind?

As I read, I drew knowledge and strength from those who had set out before us to make their own way, both in adventures and the wider context of a life. The American transcendentalist Henry David Thoreau was an obvious place to start. Rereading *Walden,* his most famous work about the two years and two months he spent living alone in a self-built cabin by Walden pond, owned by his friend and fellow transcendentalist Ralph Waldo Emerson, encouraged me to think deeply about our reasons for setting out on our own year of living differently. We, too, were rebelling against the expectations and limitations we felt so strongly, seeking a greater degree of independence and control over our day-to-day lives, striving 'to live deliberately' in Thoreau's words. As yet, we had no idea how our own experiment would change us, or what lessons we might learn about ourselves and the world around us. But the fear of staying put was far greater than the fear of this unknown. Like Thoreau, we were lucky enough to have the support of our families. But, unlike Thoreau's doting mother, they would not be doing our washing . . .

I read Michael Lanza's *Before They're Gone,* about the author's explorations in some of America's most endangered National Parks with his two children, before both children and parks changed beyond recognition. It captured the intensity of our desire to make the most of these precious times – to do everything in our power to protect those things precious to us, for as long as we had the ability to do so. And I reread an old favourite, the 1945 memoir *Space Beneath My Feet* by Gwen Moffatt – Britain's first female certified mountain guide – in which she describes the difficult early days with her daughter, Sheena, living aboard a boat and fitting in climbing when she could.

Gwen felt like something of a kindred spirit, turning her back on the expected and accepted paths, instead forging a life in the only way she knew how. Climbing barefoot, running away, living wild, funding herself through her writing among other means, the traditional gender roles of the time simply didn't make sense to her. But it was a hard struggle for her, too, battling poverty, frustration and sadness when she was unable to work or climb, while looking after her daughter, often alone.

Perhaps my favourite discovery during this time was a little-known book by Rachel Carson, best-known for her groundbreaking environmental science book, *Silent Spring*. Carson's final book, *The Sense of Wonder: A Celebration of Nature for Parents and Children*, details her wanderings along the wild coastline near her home in Maine, with her grandnephew, Roger. Published posthumously in 1965, and illustrated with photography by Nick Kelsh, it exquisitely captures the essence and importance of a life immersed in, and infused with, gratitude for the natural world, for adults and children alike. Reading this book, I realised how strongly I wanted this for our children over the coming year, and beyond. For them to be immersed in the wonder of the natural world. To explore and experience wild places at their own pace and in their own way. And also for Sim and I to be guided by E and H, rather than the other way around, learning to see and appreciate the world anew, through their eyes.

What my reading brought home to me more than anything else was that the success – or otherwise – of this adventure was up to us, along with a little luck on the side of the weather perhaps. No one else could show us the way to plan for, survive and thrive in this life we were creating for ourselves. Many people before us had sought freedom and a deeper connection – with other people, with nature – but each had, necessarily, done so in their own way.

Almost suddenly, it seemed, October was drawing to a close. The rushing impatience of time meant our thoughts were now always on the future – most immediately the first few weeks as we set out on our new way of life, and then the hazier distance beyond. We were both experiencing a strange mixture of emotions, keen to get going, anxious about the many unknowns, struggling with the idea of leaving Devon behind and driving eastwards into a busier, faster world. We were so grateful to this place that had, for the past month, been a precious refuge and an important bridge to the next stage of our adventure. We knew Dartmoor, which had mellowed to misty greys and browns over the passing weeks, would remain our safe place, wherever we were. Practically, it would also remain our postal address, which we needed in order to keep receiving our tax credits and other post. Returning to re-experience the moor for a little while each season was something we looked forward to and felt lucky to have.

So, we left the house empty and clean, as we had found it, ready for Sim's parents to move in the following week. Joining Sim and the kids in the truck, it felt at once as if a lifetime and no time at all had passed since I had locked the door of our Cotswolds house behind us a month before. But this time, the adventure felt unavoidably real. This really was the beginning of our wild year.

*

From Dartmoor we drove east, following roads that gradually became bigger and busier as we passed through Dorset and into Hampshire. Our campsite was a small, sustainably run site in the South Downs, the most south-easterly of the UK's National Parks. With a week to go before we could pick up our new bell tent, we would be using our backpacking tent, which we would keep with us for emergencies and extra space throughout the year. Having the entire field to ourselves, we picked a flat spot between high bramble hedges, sheltering us from a chill easterly wind. As we went through the familiar process of checking the ground for stones before laying out the tent it felt like we were a step closer to really being on our wild year, but I still couldn't believe it fully. Not when it all felt so much like other camping trips. Not until we had our big, new tent, which already I was thinking of as 'home'.

The site's owners were cheerful and welcoming, but it was hard to ignore the slightly sad, abandoned feel of an out-of-season campsite, so different from busy, noisy, crowded summer camping. Yet, as we pegged out the guy lines and E foraged for the last of the autumn blackberries in the hedgerows nearby, I began to wonder whether I actually preferred the quiet, melancholic atmosphere. It was easier to feel wild and adventurous when it was just us, rather than us and so many others doing the same thing.

The site was set in woodland, high on a section of the South Downs Way national trail, which traverses the country for a hundred miles between Eastbourne and Winchester. Every so often, in groups, couples or alone, walkers traipsed through the campsite, looking for the next waymarker to guide them onwards, but other than that, we had the place to ourselves.

Later that evening, wrapped in warm down jackets as supper bubbled away on our camping stove, we watched a young man walk into the site carrying a heavily loaded rucksack. Despite ours being the only other tent, he pitched right next to us and it wasn't long before he wandered over to chat. His name was Tom and, he told us in an earnest, slightly awkward tone, he had recently finished his master's degree and was taking a year out before doing a PhD. He had moved back in with his parents, which he admitted he was finding difficult, so he had decided to tick off something he had wanted to do for a while: walk the entirety of the South Downs Way, from his family home in Winchester all the way to the sea. Although he didn't say as much, we both got the impression he had set off on this adventure on an impulse, without much of a plan. I wondered if it had been a dramatic departure, or whether he had simply left without telling anyone.

When our supper was ready – a big pot of pasta and sauce steaming invitingly in the cold evening air – we expected Tom to head back to his tent. But he stayed, eyeing our food longingly, eventually admitting he had none with him. We had made plenty, so we were more than happy to share, but we wondered how he was planning to walk the remaining eighty-plus miles with no food. For the rest of the evening he talked on and on, more to himself than to us – a disjointed soliloquy that we had to interrupt when it was time to put the kids to bed. Apologising, he wandered back to his tent, vanishing into the darkness. The next morning, as we sat making porridge and planning the day ahead, we weren't surprised when he reappeared, just in time for breakfast. We had made enough for him anyway.

Those first few days in the South Downs were a strange time. It was hard to shake the feeling that we were waiting – balanced on the edge of something huge and more than a little scary. Though we were keen to discover the parts of the National Park within easy reach of our tent, it was frustrating feeling like tourists – visitors rather than the temporary yet deeply immersed residents we wanted to be. We kept busy, climbing the short but steep hills that rose above roaring roads and following pale trails that snaked into the distance across the chalk grassland. We walked to the top of Butser Hill, the highest point on the South Downs Way, and then Blackdown, the highest point in the National Park, gazing out across the Weald from Tennyson's favourite lookout at the Temple of the Winds.

We wandered through the ancient yews at Kingley Vale, their spidery boughs reaching out around them like long, jointed, bony limbs. E wound her way through the branches, climbing over and under, running around the great twisted trunks, caught up in the atmosphere of the place. Local legend tells of a fierce battle in the Vale, when the men of Chichester defeated a marauding band of Vikings over a thousand years ago. Today, the ghosts of the slaughtered Vikings are said to haunt the Yew trees, which come alive and move around on gnarled limbs at night.

And then, at long last, it was the day we were due to pick up our tent. We had all had enough of waiting: now the adventure could really begin.

Setting Sail
The Emperor and the South-East

I T WAS WELL INTO the afternoon when we arrived at our campsite, the rambling grounds of an angular, red brick backpackers' hostel, deep in the Surrey Hills Area of Outstanding Natural Beauty. It had been a painfully slow drive from the cold, grey warehouse on an industrial estate where, a few hours earlier, we had picked up the tent. Sim turned off the engine and we all sat still for a few moments, welcoming the calming silence.

On the back of our *Wild Running* book, we had been asked to write a running guide for YHA – formally the Youth Hostels Association. To help with our research, YHA had generously allowed us free camping at several of its hostels. As well as being invaluable for researching the guide, it was incredibly helpful, both as a boost to our fragile finances and because many campsites, particularly in the south-east, had already closed for the winter.

It felt good to step out into the cool air, finally freed from the noise and stress and restraints of travel. E spun wide circles through the drifts of fallen leaves, gazing up at the sky and trees that circled above her as if she was seeing all for the first time. I watched her, recognising her instinctive need to move, to explore, to locate herself in this new space. We wandered over to find the hostel's reception area to book ourselves in, but we had arrived too late and it was already closed, the whole place deserted. A sign asked us to find a pitch and come back in the morning, so we made our way back to the woods.

We walked the area, carefully checking the ground for rocks or tree stumps, steering clear of any trees that might drop their branches on our soft roof. Eventually, we settled upon a wide, flat patch of ground, large enough for our tent and surrounded by oak, beech, sweet chestnut, holly and willow.

A fine old silver birch, its trunk a pattern of deep grooves and plates like armour, stood in one corner, draped in its bright gold autumn finery. I felt, somehow, that this tree was a guardian, watching over us as we lived our lives in the woods. A pioneer species that readily re-colonises cleared land, the Celts saw the silver birch as a symbol of regeneration, of starting anew. That, at least, was what we were doing – and right at the start of the Celtic year, too.

All across the woodland floor lay a deep, soft carpet of leaves that seemed to be just waiting for our tent. After a morning filled with the busy roar of motorways it was wonderfully quiet. Though I could still hear the swish of wet tyres on a road in the distance, there in the forest a soft silence hung in the damp air, suspended like the drips of earlier rain, gathering on the thinning leaves overhead. The rustling, swaying canopy revealed glimpses of a clear, pale sky, the light already starting to fade.

We had never pitched a bell tent before, let alone an Emperor Ultimate bell tent. Keen to make the most of the day's remaining light, Sim lifted the weighty bag out of the back of the truck and carried it to the centre of the clearing, dropping it on the ground. We took the tent out of its bag and unrolled it so it lay flat across the damp grass, following the instruction sheet as we worked out how to assemble it for the first time. The whole process took over an hour on this quietly monumental evening – one that really did mark the beginning of a new phase of our lives.

As we worked, E pottered about, stroking the soft mossy bark of the trees and finding sticks to make into small piles, which she dotted around the clearing. H peered out from the warmth of his sling, often almost upside-down as I bent over to straighten the canvas or push in a peg. With big eyes, he watched his sister and the shapes of the leaves and branches as they waved gently, black against the soft grey of the evening sky. Sim put in the two big poles that provided the main support for the central part of the tent and together we pegged out the sides and guy lines, the tent growing steadily as each pole and peg went in. Then, when it was done, we all stood back to have a proper look.

'Woah – it's massive!' Sim's tone was half-admiring, half-wondering what we had done.

'I hope it fits on all the campsites . . .' I was thinking about some of the smaller places we had booked, imagining how the Emperor would look pitched next to a dozen tiny tents in the mountains.

It was *so* much bigger than we had imagined – almost embarrassingly so – towering over our heads. Unzipping the door, we stepped inside and looked around us the vastness of the space, picturing where everything would go. E pushed past and ran a full loop, arms spread out to her sides.

'Wowee!' Her voice was filled with wonder as she stopped next to us. 'It's bigger than our old house!'

We ferried our possessions through the near-dark woodland, back and forth between truck and tent. The tent carpet went down first, adding a layer of insulation on top of the heavy duty, waterproof groundsheet. Then a tough woollen rug we'd had in our house that we knew would be far warmer and more pleasant to live our daily lives upon than its synthetic underlay. This arrangement covered most of the floor space, leaving a bare section of groundsheet in front of the door for boots and wet clothing, and another at the far end where the woodburner would go. Next came our thick, striped mattresses, with basic foam camping mats underneath for extra insulation. Then two candle lanterns to hang from the ceiling poles, two beanbags and some cushions to sit on, a low camping table, the kids' patterned, quilted playmat and E's box of books and toys. Around the edge of the tent, we hoped adding extra ballast against the wind, we lined up our big, waterproof duffle bags filled with clothes and spare bedding, while at the woodburner end, we piled our heavy-duty plastic boxes filled with food and cooking utensils.

Last of all we assembled the stove, a job weighty with responsibility: we needed to cut a hole in the roof of the tent to allow the flue to pass through, carrying smoke away from our living quarters. The silicon-lined metal flashing kit we had bought would protect the canvas from heat, and prevent rain coming through, but only if we fitted it properly – and there would be no second chances. Sim took out a pen and drew a neat circle onto the blank canvas, using the inside of the metal disc as a template.

'Do you want to do it?' he asked, penknife in hand, indicating the hole that needed to be cut.

'Erm . . . I'm afraid I can't really,' I pointed to H now fast asleep in his sling on my front. 'I'd have to wake him up.'

Sim grinned and opened the largest, sharpest blade of his knife. Carefully, he pushed it through the roof of the tent and cut a perfectly round hole, following the inked line as he went. Then we fitted the flashing, screwing the two halves together with the canvas between them, and finally fed the flue through. Stepping outside, where it was now dark enough to need headtorches, we admired our handiwork – a neat chimney rising proudly from the sloping roof of the tent. We attached the fire blanket and carbon monoxide alarm to the pole nearest the stove and a fire extinguisher to a pole at the other end of the tent. Despite the success of the chimney, we decided to leave our first attempt at lighting the stove until the morning. We shared a picnic supper, the simple joy of our first meal in our new home, the light from our candle lanterns flickering on the canvas walls.

It was at once terrifying, exhilarating, joyful and a relief to finally be on our way. To be getting on with the first night – of how many, we didn't know. Apart from food, water and fuel, which we would stock up with along the way, we had everything we needed for the four of us to live for a year – or more, if we needed to.

For so long, working towards this goal, I hadn't really been able to imagine us actually *being* here, on the other side of the mountain of organising and planning. Now, at long last, I was starting to believe in our plan, to see how we might make it work.

After supper, we made our beds, adding insulating mattress protectors, blankets, duvets and more blankets. Then we walked slowly over to the washrooms to clean our teeth, E carrying her little torch, its beam picking out bright circles of the path, trees and shrubs as we went. When we were out of the woodland, with a clear view of the sky, she pointed the torch upwards, its light vanishing instantly in the impossible vastness of the night.

It felt much colder when we got back to the tent. We all wore full-length merino wool base layers to bed – and they stayed on, under our clothes, on colder days – snuggling in together as we waited for our bodies to warm the surrounding space. As we lay there, Sim reading E her bedtime story by the light of the lantern, H having his bedtime feed, a chorus of tawny owls began calling from the trees. I have never heard so many owls calling together before: it was a beautiful welcome to life in the woods. Soon both children were asleep, so we switched off the camping lantern and let the soft darkness of the outdoors night settle around us.

Two hours later, I was suddenly wide awake, my face freezing in the icy darkness. The temperature had plummeted. I listened for a moment, hearing the children's soft, rhythmic breathing, quickly checking them to make sure they were warm enough. What had woken me up? I was drifting back into sleep when I was jolted back to wakefulness by a loud clattering sound. Now Sim was awake too.

'What the hell was that?' I whispered.

We lay still, listening, every sense straining in the total blackness. Suddenly, a security light near the hostel flicked on, the light piercing straight through our pale canvas walls for a minute or so before plunging us back into darkness. It stayed off for a while and then came on again. There were more noises, too: the clank of something – or someone – knocking into the metal bin that stood on the other side of our woodland clearing . . . gravel crunching in the distance . . . rustlings from the autumn leaves . . . the faintest hint of cigarette smoke carried on the still air. The owls were silent now. It was the first time in a long time that we had experienced that primal type of fear, lying next to our precious children, nothing more than fabric between us and whatever it was outside.

'Maybe a fox?' Sim sounded unconvinced.

'Foxes don't smoke cigarettes.'

We lay there for a long time, waiting. But no other worrying sounds or smells reached our heightened senses that night. Gradually we relaxed, slipping back into sleep, every body part tucked warmly beneath layers of blanket and duvet. In all likelihood, our night-time terror had simply been a hostel resident returning late. But our overactive imaginations, fuelled by the stresses of the past months, the uncertainties to come and the ever-present question of whether this really was a responsible thing to do, had turned them into a monster.

The following morning dawned bright and cheerful, the possibility of monsters completely unimaginable. I thought back to those cold, scared hours in the night – it was hard to fully recall the terror I had felt – it all seemed slightly ridiculous now. I looked forward to a time when we were more accustomed to these things, as we surely would be before long. When the insulated existence that had been our normality before gave way to a wilder mindset, attuned to a different set of sensations.

Ravenous and in desperate need of coffee, we made our first attempt at lighting the stove, starting with dry kindling and paper and adding a couple of eco-firelighters made with vegetable oil rather than petrol as the traditional versions often are. Once that was burning well, we added some small logs, taking care not to overfill the compartment, which risked lowering the temperature too much and creating smoke. The little fire was soon crackling away, giving off a surprising amount of heat for its size, already boiling the water in its metal tank on top. I was amazed at how easy it had all been. The practicalities of using a woodburner for cooking and heating was something I'd been concerned about before we'd set out, but perhaps it wouldn't be so difficult after all.

That evening we lit the stove again, looking forward to hot food and a warm tent. We had bought a big bag of logs from a fuel station on our drive over the day before and, having used up most of the wood we had brought with us that morning, we waited until the fire was burning well and then added a couple of the new logs. Instantly there was a hissing sound and thick, yellow smoke started pouring from the front and top of the stove and into the tent. I exited quickly with E and H, taking them to the truck, out of the cold wind and smoke, while Sim battled with the damp logs. It took an hour to empty the stove, air the tent and get the fire going again, using the last of our dry wood and knowing its precious heat wouldn't last much beyond supper. We were in for a chilly evening, but it was a good lesson in the importance of using only the driest wood, and in not trusting fuel station logs which aren't necessarily as dry as they claim to be.

That first week, nestled in our sheltered patch of woodland in the Surrey Hills, we slowly began to settle into a new rhythm. First thing in the morning, often in semi-darkness, Sim and I took it in turns to brave the cold November air to light the stove, pulling on a down jacket and woolly hat and sliding silently from under the duvet so everyone else could sleep for as long as possible. First, we cleared out the ash left over from the previous day, then carefully laid a new fire on the metal base. We had taken to storing our spare wood in a pile beneath the stove, stacked and drying out, ready for use.

It usually took about half an hour for the stove to heat the tent to a bearable temperature. H, not yet mobile but now able to sit up on his own, was usually content watching the morning routine from the warmth of the bed. We had always co-slept, allowing me to feed both children as babies with as little disturbance for everyone as possible. It made even more sense in the tent, allowing us to monitor the children's body heat. E slept through the nights solidly, safe and secure between her parents, while the ability to feed H whenever he asked kept night time crying to a minimum, something I was keen to continue, particularly once campsites became busier. My nights were still a constant cycle of feeding and dozing, but I rarely felt the crushing tiredness of sleep deprivation I had experienced regularly before we left.

By the time E – never an early morning person by nature – was awake, we'd have a pot of porridge bubbling away on the stove top and water boiling for our first coffee of the day. Keeping the stove burning well took a lot of time and attention, so we often let it go out after breakfast, wrapping up in warm clothing and spending the morning working and playing with the kids. We had a big box of toys, books and building blocks to keep them occupied, which we set out in the space in the centre of the tent floor. We would swap these over for a different set each time we visited Sim's parents so they never became boring. We had a few DVDs we could watch on our laptop – the internet connection was rarely good enough for films – but, for the most part both children were happy watching everything going on both inside and outside the tent. If the weather was dry, we would take food with us and head out for the whole of the afternoon to explore. Then, in the evenings we relit the stove, warming the tent, cooking and heating more water. When absolutely necessary, we bathed the kids in a collapsible tub near to the stove, but mostly we sat around it, making the most of its precious circle of warmth before bedtime.

Just across the road from our campsite was a 2,000-acre area of wooded common land known as The Hurtwood. Though privately-owned, it was – and is – a place for all to enjoy, a right established by deed in 1926 allowing public access on foot, bike and horse. We spent hours exploring there, following sun-striped paths among towering Scots pines, slender beech and birch trees, and through a dense carpet of bilberry bushes, long since foraged by others by the time we arrived. Having always known these tiny dark fruit as either bilberries or, in Devon, whortleberries, I was amazed to discover the number of different names they are called by. Blaeberries in Scotland and the Lakes, winberries, whinberries, wimberries or whimberries in Derbyshire, fraughan in Ireland, and bulberries, trackleberries, huckleberries, windberries and myrtleberries elsewhere. These tiny wild relatives of the blueberry have been foraged for millennia across woodland, moorland and mountaintops. Packed with even more goodness than commercially grown berries, they are the ultimate free superfood.

Before we set out from Devon, one of our slightly extravagant purchases had been a candle chandelier with two tiers of tealights, a larger circle at the bottom and a smaller circle at the top, which now hung from the main pole across the top of the tent. Once we had eventually managed to get hold of enough tealights to fill all of its glass holders, we started lighting it in the evenings, enjoying the warm, mellow lighting and gentle flickering on the canvas around us.

One evening, as we sat reading to E, one of the holders exploded, showering glass onto the floor below. Fortunately, we never sat underneath the chandelier – just in case – but broken glass and children and tents were a terrifying mix. We hurriedly blew out the remaining candles, moving E and H as far away as possible so we could carefully clear up the mess and wipe down the floor to get rid of any possible splinters. The next day I rang the shop – it turned out the manufacturers were aware of the problem but it had been too expensive to use heat-proof glass. Afterwards, we sometimes lit the chandelier, placing the tealights straight into the metal cups, having emptied the useless holders into a glass recycling bin, but it never shone in quite the same way again.

*

After ten days in the Surrey Hills, we made our way west to another YHA campsite, this time near the village of Burley in the New Forest, our third National Park of the trip, including Dartmoor. We were shown to a pitch on a stretch of grass bordering the car park. It was nice and flat, and a mercifully short distance to carry everything from the truck, but it was noisy at night as people arrived and left, their car tyres crunching on the gravel and drumming over the cattle grid at the entrance. Our new pitch felt much less peaceful and hidden than our previous one had, shared as it was with other campers who came and went during the week.

The weather had also changed. Gone were the cool, dry, bright days we had grown used to and now a steady patter of rain fell on the canvas, a constant, drumming accompaniment to life. It was harder to light the stove, and we found ourselves less inclined to spend our days exploring outside when, even with waterproofs on, our clothes and boots quickly became soaked through and drying them out was a challenge. The air in the tent felt damp, even with the stove alight, as wet clothes hung from every pole. For the first time since we had set out, boredom began to set in. Sim and I longed to get out running, but our feet were already sore from days of wearing wet running shoes. The big box of books and toys, which usually worked so well as afternoon entertainment after a morning out in the fresh air, no longer held E's attention. I felt scratchy and irritable, my temper shortening with the late November days. Even H seemed less his usual sweet-natured self, perhaps picking up on the general atmosphere. But the big old manor house, which had been converted into the hostel, offered some respite. We could cook in the kitchen, with its shelves of communal-sized pans, wash our clothes in the laundry and work at the tables in the dining room rather than sitting on the tent floor.

Burley, like many of the New Forest villages we passed through, was an expensive arrangement of pretty houses and shops all in the red brick of the south-east, so different from the honey-coloured Bath Stone we had grown accustomed to in the Cotswolds. Touristy shops sold fudge and witch-themed memorabilia, the latter an echo of the village's association with 1950s celebrity white witch Sybil Leek. The weather had cleared a little, with a break in the rain, although the sky remained grey and heavy with clouds. After stopping at a food shop to buy a few things for lunch, we wandered through the village in search of a way to escape the busy road. Eventually, we found a clear track and followed it along a tree-lined ridge that climbed steadily to reach the visible earthworks of an Iron Age hillfort at the top, marked on the map as Castle Hill.

As we walked, I told E the local legend I had read of a dragon who had once upon a time lived on the hill. Each morning the dragon would fly to the nearby hamlet of Bistern for milk – for what else would a dragon have on its cornflakes? E was in good spirits, trotting along beside us, excited to be out at last after our temporary confinement in the tent. I decided not to finish the story – the part where the dragon is set upon by a misguided knight and it all ends badly.

At the top of the hill, we sat together and ate lunch. Before us, the hillside, russet with dying bracken, dropped steeply away towards the Avon Valley, where the counties of Dorset and Wiltshire meet Hampshire. I imagined those who had built the fort eyeing this view – how to them it would have meant safety, a strategic position, proximity to the abundant food and shelter of the forest. How different the south of England must have been more than 2,500 years ago, before cars and roads and industry, and when only a million people called this island home.

Back in Burley, a cow was holding up the traffic along the main road and hairy ponies grazed the verges. They seemed in strange juxtaposition to the smart houses and expensive cars, which roared past, apparently oblivious to the many signs warning of collisions with these gentle animals. According to the website of the Verderers, the voice of the New Forest Commoners, around ninety animals belonging to Commoners, including ponies, donkeys, cattle, pigs and sheep, are killed in vehicle collisions each year, mostly the victims of local drivers. More than a hundred deer, which are classed as wild animals, are also killed on the New Forest's roads every year. Reading the statistics made me shudder.

The majority of the New Forest National Park, like much of Dartmoor, and 3 per cent of England as a whole, is covered by ancient Commoners' Rights. First laid out in the Charter of the Forest in 1217, these rights include: *pasturage* – the right to graze animals; *pannage* – the right to put pigs out to feed on acorns; *estover* – the right to take firewood; and *piscary* – the right to take fish. I enjoyed these unfamiliar old words and the sense of connection with people and place going back centuries. We also discovered the historic law of *perambulation* – the act of walking a parish to delineate its boundaries, which is still practised in this part of England. More appropriately to us, the word also describes the movement, by people, of passing or wandering through or over the land. This was how we wanted to come to know the places we stayed at – perambulating, at the pace of a small child, stopping frequently, taking in each detail of texture, sight, sound and smell along the way.

Three weeks into our new life under canvas we were gradually becoming accustomed to using the woodburner – the twice-daily routine of cleaning, lighting and keeping it alive for as long as we needed its warmth. The top plate was just large enough to fit two saucepans, but I was delighted to discover that, by using a tiered steamer, we could cook rice or pasta in the base and vegetables on top, maximising the available space and heat. Breakfast was usually porridge, and supper some arrangement of pasta, curries, soups and stews, using fresh ingredients we bought as we went combined with our staple supply of tinned beans or chickpeas, stock, herbs or spices and garlic. It all felt warming and wholesome and there was always chocolate afterwards. Even at breakfast.

E had as much as she wanted of whatever we were having; now, at six months old, H was starting to do the same. I loved watching his expressions as he explored different foods, often with his hands first. Having only drunk milk for his entire life, I couldn't imagine what this experience of tasting different flavours for the first time must be like. We wanted to leave him to explore this new culinary world in his own time as much as possible, within the limits of our ability to wash and dry everything, so we dressed him in a waterproof smock at mealtimes, which we could rinse and hang out to dry afterwards. We placed morsels of food on his tray and he experimented, tasting banana, porridge, dal and yoghurt, or contemplating a handful of stewed apple or a breadstick. He would watch his sister carefully, often copying what she did. He loved it when she played with him. Their favourite game – E hiding behind her hands before popping out with a loud 'BOO!' – sent him into helpless fits of laughter.

We had no easy way of cooking bread and, while we sometimes bought fresh baguettes when we came across them, loaves were expensive to buy and hard to keep fresh. So I made flatbreads, putting a basic bread dough to rise in a basin by the fire then stretching it into circles and cooking it in a dry frying pan. These where amazingly versatile and we dipped them into soup; folded and filled them like sandwiches; or even turned them into simple pizzas. E enjoyed helping, shaping her own little ball of dough on a floured plate, which I would then cook for her.

Meals were cosy, happy times, sitting on cushions on the floor around our little camping table, topped with a wooden board and a wipe-clean tablecloth, all a perfect height for the kids. We kept our food supplies in our waterproof storage boxes – all the essentials including porridge oats, rice, pasta, flour, dried and tinned pulses, stock cubes, dried herbs and spices, oils, vinegar, salt, sugar and yeast. We kept a close eye on these stores and topped them up regularly. Keeping food cold was easy over the winter months, when the air temperature was often near freezing, but when the weather was warmer, we would have to be careful to buy food that needed to be kept cool only in small quantities that we used quickly. With our budget so tight, we bought food little and often so we never wasted anything.

There were so many areas of life that we'd had to simplify in order to take them with us on this trip: we had no room for a buggy or a highchair, so we carried the children on our fronts or backs and sat H on our laps at mealtimes. There was no fridge to peruse for snacks, no heater to flick on for a quick blast of warmth, and no sofa to relax on in the evenings. But, strangely, we didn't think of any of these absences as hardships – it never felt as though we were living under that crushing weight of austerity that we had left behind – instead, there was a sense of pulling together to make it work, and, most importantly, the knowledge that we were so much more in control of our lives.

*

We were enjoying discovering the south-east but, deep within my soul I yearned for wilder, more peaceful places, free from the constant background roar of traffic and where nature and human activity seemed not always to be so much at odds with each other. Our plan was to gradually make our way back west, aiming to arrive in Cornwall during the first week of December. To break our journey we had arranged to camp at a farm overlooking the sea on East Devon's Jurassic Coast, designated a UNESCO World Heritage Site for its extraordinary geology.

Leaving the New Forest, we took the quiet road that hugs the coastline, winding our way through Dorset's sleepy villages, already deep in their winter hibernation. We arrived at the farm in late afternoon sunshine, a gentle breeze, lightly salted by the sea, blowing dry leaves in eddies around the yard. H had been restless in the car, so I unclipped him from his seat and took him with me to the site office to knock on the door. It was opened by a thick-set man in a waxed jacket, cap and wellies.

'Hello,' he boomed, looking me up and down, and then over my head as if I wasn't what he was looking for at all.

Slightly taken aback, I glanced behind me. 'Uhm . . . hi. We're here to camp – we've been chatting over email . . .'

'Oh, I know who you are.' He spoke with a strong West country accent in a voice so loud that every time he spoke it made H cry. '*You're* the mad camping people! Where's your husband?'

As if I wasn't there, he strode past me and over to where Sim was getting out of the truck. It turned out (he was keen to tell Sim) that our truck was the same model as his, only a decade or so older. After pumping Sim's hand enthusiastically, he showed us the way across the yard to the field where we would be camping.

'Completely mad!' he shouted as he set off. H burst into tears again.

He opened the gate and made a wide, sweeping gesture that took in the sloping field beyond. 'Take your pick! The best views are from the top. It's going to be windy, mind.' That booming laugh again.

He made as if to go, then stopped, as if a thought had occurred to him. Turning back to us, he added: 'I'll leave the little caravan at the end unlocked just in case you need it – you never know!'

It was a kind gesture in its way – he knew better than most the force of the winds that scoured these fields, straight off the sea – but the hint of mockery in his voice was hard to ignore, even if I was too busy comforting H to make much of it. After he strode off across the field back to the warmth of his house, the world seemed incredibly quiet.

We walked together around the field, searching for the flattest spot to pitch the tent, eventually settling on a place at the top, tucked into the corner of two dense hedges, with far-reaching views of the spectacular Jurassic coastline and a calm blue sea, sparkling beneath a sinking sun. It was a still evening, warm for November. After we had pitched the tent, we sat outside with E and H on our laps, watching as the sea and sky blazed pink and orange, gradually fading to dusky purple, then darkening to a deep blue.

Later on, the wind picked up and began buffeting the tent. Inside, the stove was alight and burning well. As each week passed it felt as though we were learning how to work with it to get it to burn best – how to use small pieces of the driest wood we could find, to leave the little front hatch open just a crack to get it hot enough for cooking and then shut it tightly afterwards so it would stay warm for as long as possible. Sitting together over supper it felt wonderful to be cosy, warm and dry inside the tent, listening to the weather outside yet completely protected.

Suddenly there was a loud BANG. We all stopped eating and looked at one another. E darted over to sit next to H on my lap while Sim stood up and went outside to see what had happened. The noise turned out to have been a tent peg exploding out of the ground and hitting one of the poles, the force of its sudden release making the sound of metal against metal incredibly loud. Sim replaced the peg, carefully checking all the others as he did so. Bedtime came and went with no further explosions, but we spent the rest of the night watching the tent walls heaving and the poles shuddering and bending, taking it in turns to brave the gale every so often to push pegs back in.

The pegs were not the only problem. Wanting to make the most of the view, we had pitched the tent with the main entrance facing into the wind, which now blew straight in off the sea, forcing rain through the zip and onto our floor. There was little we could do until the morning, other than move everything clear and put a towel down to soak up the growing puddle. Air spilled through other gaps, too, filling the space inside the tent until we could actually feel the pressure building. Then the next gust would hit with a bang as the air was forced back out again. Each time this happened we lay still in the dark, waiting, wondering. Could the tent take such a battering? Or was it about to collapse on top of us?

The morning found us with bruised hands and a circle of small craters around the tent where pegs had been dragged out and pushed back in over and over again. But, to our relief, the tent had stood its ground against the wind. As soon as the rain stopped, we dragged it down the hill to a more sheltered spot and angled the door away from the view and the wind. Another important lesson learnt.

The next few days were cold but dry, plentiful sunshine filling the inside of our bright canvas bell tent with warmth and light. One afternoon, as I sat watching E playing while H slept in the crook of my arm, I gazed up at the gently waving shadow patterns as sunlight filtered through the branches of a nearby tree. I loved these temporary paintings on the blank canvas of our tent – a different picture in every place, at every time of year, whenever the sun shone. Far below, beyond the village with its thatched cottages and narrow lanes, I could hear the rhythmic wash of waves on a pebble shore. It was one of those rare moments, pinned into stillness by a sleeping child and with no urgent chores or work to be done, when I could simply exist and enjoy that warm, together feeling of *now*.

We made the most of the November sunshine, exploring the wide arc of the bay that curved away to either side of the little village below our campsite. We walked barefoot on the beach, feeling the smooth, sun-warmed pebbles on our skin, daring the icy water to wash over our toes. One morning, finding the rolling East Devon landscape bright, fresh and sparkling in the sunshine after a night of rain, we climbed the steep path up to the cliff top high above the beach. I had H in his sling on my front while E rode high on Sim's shoulders. Even with E and a heavy pack, Sim quickly opened up a big gap between us, his powerful legs allowing him to stride seemingly effortlessly up the hillside. But I didn't mind. Sim might be gifted with acceleration and speed that can literally leave me standing, but I'm an economical runner and can go a long way on very little. He can always beat me in shorter races but, in the past, when we have run marathons together, I often have the edge in the later stages. This gently competitive rivalry is one of the many things I love about our relationship.

Eventually, I joined him on the plateau of grassy common land at the top, the hills and the coast opening out in layers of green and gold and blue before us. Looking down into the wide bay before us, we spotted a pod of harbour porpoises, arching through the water not far from the cliffs below. We watched, completely entranced, jointly entering that state of mind where nothing else – not even ourselves – existed for us for those few, magical moments.

As November drew to a close, with only three nights of our week-long stay remaining, the sky turned dark grey and ragged with storm clouds – a stern warning of the rapid approach of winter. From our pitch high up on the headland, I looked down at the sea with a sense of trepidation: its gunmetal grey opacity; its rugged, wind-whipped, white-tipped surface; all so different from the serene blue calmness of the previous days. That evening, the rain started to fall with ominous persistence and the wind grew steadily stronger. Sim was busy getting the stove ready to light to cook our evening meal, but every gust shook the tent violently, rattling the flue where it passed through the tent roof.

'I don't like this.' There were lines of concern on his usually cheerful face.

'No.' I listened to the gathering sounds of the wind outside, remembering the ease with which it had wrenched the tent pegs from the earth only days earlier. 'We could just have a picnic rather than lighting the stove – to be on the safe side.'

'Or . . .' He hesitated, as if weighing the situation, the weather, our finances. 'We could go to the pub?'

I didn't need a second invitation. We pulled on slightly smarter clothes, packed waterproofs for all of us and ran over to the truck through horizontal rain. Just before we drove off, Sim ran back to push the pegs in firmly and check all the zips and vents were firmly closed. We didn't want to take any chances.

The force of the rain was almost painful by the time we reached the thatched pub in the centre of the village and we parked the truck and ran for the door. Eating out was a rare luxury for us: on a budget of £10 per night on accommodation for the year, and as little as possible on everything else, it was something we usually saved for special occasions. But as the rain and gales hammered the south coast that night, we had no regrets about our decision: it felt like a much safer and more enjoyable alternative to cooking in the tent.

We spent the evening sharing delicious food in a warm, bright room by a crackling open fire, chatting with friendly strangers, luxuriating in having someone else to cook, bring food and wash up for us, making it all last as long as we could before going back out there to brave the storm. Eventually, long after E and H had dozed off on our laps, we draped our waterproof jackets over them and hurried them into their car seats. The rain was still torrential and the wind gathered force as we drove back up the hill, winding our way along the narrow country lanes, the beam of our headlights bouncing off a wall of water ahead of us.

Grateful for the truck and its rugged competence in such conditions, I thought back to the warmth and cheerful chatter of the pub, enjoying the rare feeling of being slightly too full, looking forward to snuggling up in our big, cosy bed. I turned to Sim.

'I'm so glad we went out – it was such a lovely evening.'

He placed a hand on my thigh. 'It was.' Overhead, the branches of the trees reaching across the lane swayed and bowed in the wind. The lane was littered with snapped twigs, which pinged off the underneath of the truck as we went. 'Definitely the right decision.'

Reaching the top of the hill, we turned off the lane and into the farmyard, which now had a river flowing through it.

'Wow – it's a lot worse that it was when we left.' I could hear concern in Sim's voice as we bumped over the rough ground and through the open gateway. 'I hope the tent's ok.'

But as soon as the beam of the headlights picked out the pale canvas shape at the far side of the field it was clear the tent was not ok. That, in fact, something was horribly wrong. Our canvas mansion, usually so magnificent in its size and symmetry, looked flattened and misshapen. As we drew up in front of it, the scale of its destruction became even clearer.

Leaving E and H sleeping in their car seats, we ran through the lashing rain, unzipping the front door to reveal the full extent of the damage in the beams of our torches. Inside was a scene of utter chaos and destruction, barely recognisable as the neatly arranged home we had left behind earlier that evening. Both main poles had snapped in half, others had bent, and the end of the tent where our sleeping quarters had been had completely disappeared beneath the heavy, sagging roof, which had collapsed inwards. At first I could barely process what it meant. All I could think of was an immense, overwhelming sense of relief that we hadn't been inside with the stove alight when it happened. Then it hit me: there was no way we could salvage this. No way we could continue camping as we had been. And no way we could afford to start again. It was exactly a month since we had set out on our big adventure and already it was over.

'Jen – you take the kids and wait in the caravan.'

While I had been frozen to the spot, almost unable to understand what had happened, Sim was instantly analysing and dealing with the situation. The urgency in his voice jolted me back to the present, to the need to do something, right now, to begin the process of fixing it. 'I'll pack all this into the truck and then I'll come and join you. Then we can work out what to do next.'

I remembered my indignation only a few days earlier at the farmer's suggestion we might not know what we were taking on. Now the caravan was our only option. The storm was furious, engulfing, wind and rain beat at the hills, the houses and the crumpled remains of our tent, hurling itself from the sea which roared violent and thundering in the bay below.

I ran back to the truck and wrapped E and H back up in waterproof jackets. Then I picked up E, carrying her across to the little door in the side of the caravan, hoping with all my heart that it really would be unlocked. To my relief, the door opened easily and, a moment later, we were inside, half-falling into the stale, musty air of a space that hadn't been used for a long time. E was awake now, asking questions, oblivious to the chaos outside. I settled her onto the bed and told her I'd be back with H in a minute. As I went to collect him, I swung my torch beam over the tent, but Sim was nowhere to be seen. He was in there somewhere, wrestling with the wreckage of our recent existence. Hurrying back to the caravan with H, who by now was also wide awake and crying, I shut the door on the storm, finally quieting its furious roar.

Settling us all on the narrow bed, I held the kids close, feeding H and talking softly to E. Soon they were both asleep again, two blonde heads, one curly, one straight, snuggled up against me. I pulled a blanket over us, feeling the chill of damp clothes seeping through to our skin. The caravan rocked and groaned, swaying when the wind caught it as if we were out at sea. From far below came the sound of real waves, battering the coast and the pebble beach where we had walked together just that morning. I thought of Sim, out there in the darkness. I thought of all our stuff – everything we needed to survive the winter to come – clothing, cooking equipment, food, bedding, heating, entertainment – all wrapped up in that huge, sodden, canvas mess. I thought of the split-second decision that had meant we weren't in the tent with the stove alight, when it had collapsed.

The minutes crawled by as the weather roared outside. The dim light of the bedside lamp threw strange shadows onto the walls. Tired furniture stood around a small TV. Stained lino flooring showed the wear of decades of past inhabitants' holiday routines. The door rattled, making me jump – a brief moment of hope that it might be Sim, somehow finished already – but it was just the wind. I longed to be out there, helping him, but I couldn't move, pinned to the spot by the need to let the kids sleep. Fear and doubt clawed at my mind: how could this have happened already, only two months into our year-long adventure? What were we doing, putting our children through this madness when they could be settled somewhere with a roof and walls that didn't blow away at the first storms of the year?

Hours later, the door handle turned, and Sim blew in with the storm – a sudden fury of sound and cold air that blasted into the muffled quiet of the caravan. He was breathing heavily, so wet that a puddle was already forming around him; his face was clouded with worry and exhaustion.

'I think we're all packed.'

'Is it salvageable?' I asked, trying to tell from his face whether there was any hope of carrying on.

'I don't know – some of it, maybe. It's hard to tell.'

We talked briefly about staying until morning, but without our bedding and so little chance of sleep anyway in this rocking, rattling van we both knew the only real option was to head back to Dartmoor. Back to the door that would always be open for us in times like this – I just wished we hadn't needed to use it quite so soon. We wrapped our sleeping children back up and carried them to the truck, fastening them into their seats, tucking blankets around them and kissing them goodnight as if it were just another normal evening. They both awoke briefly but, by the time the truck had rolled across the rough ground to the lane for the final time, they were fast asleep. Then we drove west through the night to Devon, now the nearest thing we had to a home.

*

We arrived in Dartmoor just as the first glow of dawn began to pale the black edges of the moorland sky. Sim had phoned his parents before we left, letting them know we were on our way but not to wait up. Leaving everything in the truck apart from our sleeping bags and camping mats, which had been safely packed away in a waterproof duffle bag and had therefore escaped damage in the storm, we crept into the house and made a bed for us all on the floor of the living room, exactly where we had slept a month before. So tired we could barely think, in a place that, after the storm and the drive, felt like a haven of comfort and warmth, we slept soundly until late the next morning. We had many things to sort out before we could continue our trip, but these – and the many questions that would be asked – could wait.

It was hard not to feel despondent as we dragged everything out of the truck and tried to find places to hang it all out to dry. We were lucky that no rain was forecast for the next week, so we spread the tent out in the little field behind the cottage and spent hours sorting through kit, drying out or mending what we could and ordering replacements for the few things that were beyond salvage. In the end, the destruction wasn't as bad as we had feared. The company we had bought the tent from kindly agreed to send us replacement pegs and poles for free. They would be with us in a week and we planned to be ready to go as soon as they arrived.

Now that Sim's parents had moved into to the cottage, the house wasn't big enough for us all, so each night, we took our backpacking tent, mats and sleeping bags and wild camped on the moor nearby. Our favourite spot was completely hidden from view, tucked away beneath an outcropping of granite boulders. Wild camping is permitted on certain parts of Dartmoor, but only for one or two nights at a time, and we didn't want anyone, or a curious cow or pony, stumbling upon our tent in our absence. It only took a few minutes to pitch, so we took it down each morning and put it back up at bedtime.

We had arrived back on Dartmoor feeling sad and a little humiliated at such a disaster befalling us so early on in our trip. But the place soon started to work its magic on us. At night, snug in our tiny tent, warmed by the heat of our bodies, we were soothed by the sounds of the surrounding moor. In the day we explored, revisiting places we'd got to know the month we left. Trailing E along sheep tracks lined with gorse that grew higher than her head, we often met small gatherings of Dartmoor ponies, grazing the rough grass or sheltering in the lee of the rocky tors. Watchful through long, dense forelocks that hung over bright, brown eyes, they reached velvet noses towards us, blowing warm, grass-scented breath on our hands and faces. On cold mornings we found them in larger groups, huddled together for warmth, surrounded by their own steamy clouds. E and H both loved these encounters, squealing with excited joy as a soft nose with its prickly whiskers approached, nuzzling hopefully at pockets in search of food. But we were careful never to feed them, not to encourage them to seek out people in places where they might put themselves in danger.

And if ever we were in doubt that we should keep going, there was the hopeful sign that work was getting busier, now that we had more time to dedicate to it, with requests for our writing and photography and invitations to speak at events coming in. While it felt strange to be dealing with these smart, professional worlds when spent much of our time so disconnected from anything remotely corporate, it was something we were gradually becoming used to. We had a spare, clean, neatly folded set of clothes for each of us, flat packed in the truck for special occasions. Talks, meetings with publishers, interviews, photoshoots – it was essential we didn't look – or smell – like we lived in a tent. We were acutely aware of the possibility of judgement and presumption from others, having made the decision to live wild – not as a romantic, care-free couple, but professionals and parents in our thirties. The kids though, came with us when we went to meetings – there was no alternative. I was always so grateful that the people we worked with were without exception encouraging and accommodating, whether I needed to breastfeed halfway through a meeting or deliver talks with H in his sling on my front. At one particularly important meeting, H managed to completely charm a lovely publisher. It wasn't the standard way of doing things but it seemed to be working – and it was all part of our new life, the new adventure of all being together.

WINTER

'I am out with lanterns, looking for myself'

Emily Dickinson.

Festivities
Christmas under canvas in the Blackdown Hills

D URING THE SECOND WEEK of December, our new tent poles arrived. We had mended, replaced or decided we could do without everything else that had been damaged in the storm. Now we were ready to set out again, we knew we would take many important lessons from our experience. Never again would we underestimate the power of the wind, the importance of pitching at the right angle or the wisdom of a gut instinct. And never again would we mistake the Emperor's size for strength – when it came down to it, the vast sheet of canvas had acted more like a sail than a fortress.

This episode had cost us a couple of hundred pounds we could ill afford and also forced a change in our plans. Our original intention had been to head from the Jurassic Coast eastwards into Cornwall to camp on a small farm that offered glamping over the summer months. But now, with Christmas fast approaching, they were no longer able to accommodate us. I began a frantic search for alternatives. Our hidden pitch beneath the hedge near to Sim's parents' house or, when the weather allowed, our wild camping spot on the moor, crammed into our tiny backpacking tent, were rapidly becoming unworkable. And, though they were always so welcoming, and it was wonderful to watch E and H enjoying some unexpected extra time with their grandparents, we couldn't keep imposing on Sim's poor parents and their tiny cottage, currently filled to the rafters with our stuff.

Eventually, I found a small year-round campsite in the Blackdown Hills Area of Outstanding Natural Beauty. I had once lived for a while in a rented house on the edge of the Blackdowns, which mark the border between Devon and Dorset. I remembered running through a rolling landscape of farmland and woodland and the leg-sapping nature of the deceptively steep-sided hills. Cut through by the River Culm, which twists and loops its way south to join the Exe, it is one of those rare remaining corners of England that still feels genuinely undiscovered, passed by on the M5 between the Midlands and the beaches of Devon and Cornwall. The helpful, accommodating owner, after hearing what we were doing, offered us a generous discount on his usual rates.

It was exciting to be off again, Sim loading the truck while his mum and I drank tea and kept the kids entertained. And thankfully, it was only a short drive to our new pitch. We arrived to find the site peaceful and empty, and followed the cheerful owner to a small field at the bottom of a hill, edged by a plantation of young silver birches, bare and twiggy in their winter attire. He showed us around, pointing out washrooms, drinking water and electricity points, and we thanked him, feeling grateful and fortunate to have found somewhere that seemed so perfectly suited to our needs.

I think we were both a little nervous as we pitched the Emperor for the first time since our disastrous night on the Jurassic Coast. It brought back many of the emotions of that night and the days immediately afterwards: anxieties about the harshness of this way of life; the weight of responsibility to keep our children safe; our vulnerability in the face of the unpredictable British weather. But I also felt proud of our resilience: here we were, back out on our adventure, having repaired and replaced our damaged kit, and with even more experience to fall back on should we need to again, as well as a doubly renewed gratitude for our generous and supportive families. Overall, the experience had taught us many lessons we wouldn't forget in a hurry.

We slotted in the new poles, pegged out the guy lines and assembled the stove, then stepped back to have a proper look. The pale canvas was a little muddied in places, but other than that it all looked pretty much as it had before. It was a huge relief. We also had an exciting new addition to our camping setup – an inner tent, which we had spotted while waiting for our poles, much reduced in price due to what the seller referred to as 'extensive damage'. We decided to risk it. When it arrived, it was missing some of the loops that fixed it to the main tent, and had a small rip in one wall, but these were all easily fixed and now it all worked perfectly. Hanging in one corner of the main tent, taking up about a quarter of our living space, our new bedroom was a revelation. The extra layer of fabric between us and the outside world made it so much warmer. And it meant we could keep our bedding and clothes separate from our living area, well away from muddy boots and the perpetual stickiness of tiny hands.

For the first time since we had set out, we paid the extra £2 per night for electric hook-up, which felt like a real luxury. We had borrowed a small convection heater, which we plugged into the campsite supply with an extension lead. The first time we switched it on, just before bedtime on that first, chilly December evening in the Blackdown Hills, we couldn't believe how quickly it warmed up our sleeping quarters. Over the days that followed, it felt incredible to come back from a cold walk and have heat at the simple flick of a switch, rather than the time-consuming process of getting the woodburner going. If it was really cold, one of us sat in the warmth of the bedroom with the kids, while the other lit the stove to warm up the rest of the tent. With our big duvets and blankets and the new heater, which we could leave on low overnight, our sleeping quarters were suddenly unrecognisably cosy. While we had embraced the simplification of life, and the removal of many of these instant fixes from our days, being able to warm up cold children – and ourselves – so quickly was something we now had a whole new level of appreciation for.

Having electricity in the tent also meant we could keep everything – laptop, camera, phones, lights, speakers – fully charged, rather than having to ration their use and constantly search for places to plug it all in. Without hook-up, Sim would often leave me to work in a café, surrounded by charging electrical equipment, while he took the kids exploring for an hour or two. But this was expensive and inconvenient. We could now also listen to music every evening without worrying about running down the batteries in our little speaker. Music changed the whole experience of an evening in the tent – lifting a sombre mood, soothing a fractious one or bringing joy, laughter and silliness by getting us all singing and dancing.

My parents are professional musicians so I grew up in a house that was always filled with music. My dad toured the world, playing in jazz bands, and both of my parents played in classical orchestras, so the soundtrack to my childhood was a diverse one. Music was so much a part of my upbringing that in a way I wasn't even aware of it: all my parents' friends were professional musicians; their jobs and their social lives revolved around music – I couldn't imagine life any other way. I loved playing in bands and youth orchestras growing up. I wasn't bad, but neither was I disciplined enough at practising to be really good. I'd do just about enough, then get fidgety and go out on my bike. But that deep connection with music is something I feel lucky to have and is one that I want to pass onto E and H. I hope they choose to play an instrument one day and can experience that unity of consciousness and uplifting of the heart that comes from making music with other people.

Some evenings after supper, we would sit with the lantern casting shadow patterns on the canvas, the last embers of the stove glowing warm in the darkness, and music filling the tent and rising into the night all around us. People have often asked how we managed the long, dark evenings of the winter months. We made our own entertainment, or sometimes, taking our cues from the natural world, we were all asleep by seven.

*

Gunshots ripped through the quiet darkness of the night, dragging me from the depths of a dream, surfacing into a state of confusion. Had it really been gunshots – or had I dreamt it? Perhaps a branch had fallen from a tree. Or a car had backfired. I lay still and listened, feeling my heart rate gradually return to normal. Nothing. Of course it wasn't gunshots.

But then they came again – two sharp cracks, shattering the peace, and my illusions.

'What the . . .?' Sim was awake now, although thankfully the kids were still sleeping. 'Was that a gun?'

'I think so,' I whispered into the darkness. 'That's the second time I've heard it.'

Neither of us had any idea what to do. This wasn't a scenario we had ever considered while planning for our wild year. We certainly didn't want to draw attention to our presence, so we just kept quiet and waited. I couldn't decide whether or not I should be afraid, finding myself more intrigued than anything. Lying there, waiting for the next gunshot, took me back to the military exercises we were made to take part in at school. The school had a Combined Cadet Force, compulsory unless you were a conscientious objector, and I joined the army for no better reason than because I liked the colour of the uniform. At sixteen, we learnt to field strip an L98A2 Cadet GP rifle, clean it, and put it back together again. We learnt to shoot, lying on our fronts in the mud and firing at carboard cut-outs, something I discovered, slightly to my disgust, that I was excellent at. Sometimes they'd take us out into the woods after dark to ambush each other with blanks. I loathed it all – the shouting, the discipline, the ironing – and, after a year of rebelling, was dishonourably discharged and went to play chamber music instead. But not before I'd achieved a perfect score in marksmanship.

Back in the tent that night in the Blackdown hills there were no more shots, although a short while later we heard the sounds of low voices and boots crunching on gravel close to the tent. At some point I must have fallen asleep, waking hours later to bright daylight and a sense of sleep-deprived confusion.

The following day, as I searched for phone signal near the top of the site where most of the caravans and campervans were parked, an older man emerged from a battered van and walked towards me, a small brown dog at his heels. I raised a hand and said hello. He looked a little rough, as if he had been wearing the same clothes for a long time, but as he got nearer I saw kind, smiling eyes beneath his old woolly hat. He seemed to want to talk, soon embarking on a story about the job he used to do – twenty years of stress and meetings until, in the end, he had walked out and moved into a van with his dog.

'I'm happy now,' he told me, with a rueful smile. 'Lord of my own life. Not a fool anymore, working for those people. Make enough for what I need with washing up and odd jobs. Plus,' he gave me a wink, 'there's plenty of food about, if you know where to look.'

Thinking back to our disturbed night, I wondered whether one of the local pheasants, of which there were hundreds in the lanes, fields and woods nearby, had supplemented his food budget that week. I despised the whole culture of game shooting: the animal cruelty; the use, by the elite few, of land that should be for everyone to enjoy; the arrogance of those who called it a sport. But part of me enjoyed the idea of those who had so little – demanded so little – benefitting from it all in some way. Like Danny and his dad in Roald Dahl's *Danny the Champion of the World*.

*

Christmas was fast approaching, and yet this year we felt such a long way away from the usual frenzy of last-minute shopping and awkward parties. The brightly coloured lights and decorations in the nearby towns seemed gaudy and distracting when we went to buy supplies after spending a week in the chill quiet of our little field. In truth, we were delighted to have escaped it all.

This would be the first year that E really understood enough about Christmas to get excited about it, and H's first ever, which was exciting for all of us. Our little potted Christmas tree, which we bought the year E was born, was being well looked after at my dad and stepmum's house while we had no place to put it. Instead, we brought in a few feathery branches of pine from the nearby woods, scenting the tent with the tangy, resinous greenness of Yuletide. We added a few decorations that we had brought with us, and some more that we made with E from tiny larch cones and seashells. We tucked sprigs of holly and mistletoe behind the poles and wound fairy lights along their length which brought a festive cheer to our evenings. My sister had made us a string of bunting – the traditional decoration for a bell tent – and we put this up last, looping it around the front door. Whenever I caught a glimpse of its cheerful patterns, I thought of her and the ridiculous, giggling excitement of our childhood Christmases, and it warmed my heart.

Meanwhile, there was the rain. The week before Christmas, it rained almost unceasingly – a constant, heavy drumming on the canvas that filtered into every moment, waking or sleeping. A sea of mud stretched from the tent door, trampled and churned by the regular coming and going of our feet. I lamented the steady encroachment of mud into every part of our lives – it was impossible to escape from, all the more frustrating given how hard it was to wash and dry anything. One morning, Sim dragged over some sturdy wooden pallets he had spotted in a pile at the edge of the site and arranged them into a raised walkway across our deepening quagmire. It worked brilliantly, instantly changing the whole experience of entering and leaving the tent into something enjoyable, rather than nightmarish. We now also had a dry place to leave our boots outside the tent, sheltered from the rain by the tarp, pitched over the front door as a porch. Our sturdy, Gore-tex-lined walking boots had become essential whenever we were outside the tent. It was so familiar it was almost an unconscious process, pulling them on and winding the laces tight every time we ventured out. Our boots gave us grip on slippery ground, waterproofing up to our ankles and proved a useful tool for kicking stones away from the tent or pushing in pegs. They were an important part of my psychological armour, too: with my boots on I felt ready to tackle anything.

The shower block, a short walk away from our tent across a stretch of grass and a rough track, had been renovated at the end of the camping season, ready for visitors once the warmer weather arrived. It was gleaming and immaculate, more like a hotel bathroom than one on a campsite. How we treasured it. Hot water gushed with warm generosity from the showers, filling the cubicle with steam and glorious heat. It was always so hard to leave, the icy air creeping in as soon as the shower was switched off; warm, damp skin instantly freezing into goosebumps. When I took E along with me, I froze even more, making sure she was completely dry and dressed before attending to myself. We were so worried about sullying this pristine building with our big muddy boots that we took a spare pair of clean shoes with us whenever we went, changing into, and out of them at the door; it felt like the least we could do, given our generous discount and having the run of the place. And keeping as many parts of our lives free from mud as possible felt worth any amount of effort.

At times it did feel as though we were constantly on the search for a good laundrette. These became both a necessity and even a thing to look forward to, particularly when it was cold and rainy outside. We would bag up all our washing and file into the nearest laundrette, often filling up several machines at a time. E loved to post in the coins, and then we'd all settle down in the warm, soap-scented room to watch the washing go round, our faces peering back at us from the round glass windows. Before this trip, I had not been in a laundrette for years. Most were far more pleasant than the ones I remembered from my bedsit days, when the local one smelled of a vile melee of unwashed clothes and the Chinese takeaway next door. These days, though, we sat in a clean, smart shop, enjoying the heat and the simple necessity to wait, a relaxing contrast to the usual constant need to get things done. On a few occasions, when the weather was good, Sim took the kids off for an adventure while I managed a couple of hours of uninterrupted work, the washing tumbling away in the background.

Stephen King once wrote that, when all else fails, one should give up and go to the library. It is sound advice and, on such wet weeks, that's what we did. There was almost always a library nearby. Some were brand new – clean, modern buildings with colourful, cushioned children's sections. Others were tired and grey, dog-eared as the well-loved paperbacks that filled their shelves, reminding me of the library I knew and loved as a child. But each and every library was a sanctuary – somewhere we could go to be warm, dry and comfortable, where no one noticed how long we stayed or how many books we read while we were there. Some even offered organised activities for kids and, if we were lucky and managed to time it right, E and H could join in with crafting sessions, singing or storytime. It felt wondrous that we could access all of this for free. As Zadie Smith observes in her brilliant book of essays, *Feel Free*: libraries are the only things left on the high street that don't want either your soul or your wallet.

*

It was Christmas Eve, after a night of gales, when the rain finally stopped. H had woken early, wanting to be up and playing, picking up on the general pre-Christmas excitement. My first thought, when I awoke with sleep still clawing at my mind, was how quiet the world seemed – textured and layered with peaceful sounds that had been drowned out by days of hammering rain. A thrush was singing its twice-over tune from a nearby tree, announcing the dawn chorus to come, but as yet it was still quite dark, the first paling of sunrise just visible through the tent wall.

It had been days since I'd last managed to go for a run. The rain and mud and the lengthy process of getting everyone out in the fresh air and then drying everything out afterwards had been enough on its own, without adding extra mud and sweat to the mix. But now I was desperate. Leaving a fully awake, overexcited H and a sleeping E with Sim, I dressed warmly, adding a hat and gloves before unzipping the tent onto a cold, blue dawn. Pausing for a moment, I breathed in huge lungfuls of cold, clear air; delighting at the breeze on my face, rejoicing at the change in the weather and the freedom it bestowed upon my morning. As I set off up the narrow lane, unable to control my excitement, I spread my arms wide and whooped with joy.

To the east, the sky was a pale blue, tinted with yellow, hinting at the place where the sun would soon rise. Above the horizon hung Venus, gleaming silver, bright over the ink-black silhouettes of distant hills and bare trees. The western sky was still dark, studded with glittering stars, but none so bright and constant as the morning star. It felt so good to move freely, and I stretched my arms above my head, making big circles, every part of me feeling tight and restricted after days of crouching and kneeling and carrying children.

Alert to everything, as I neared a stand of woodland, I became aware of a presence within the trees – something watching me from the dense tangle of ivy and bramble. At first, I could only see an outline: two perfectly triangular pointed ears above a dark face, the body sinking into inky shadow below. Gradually

I became aware of eyes, meeting my gaze, steady and unafraid. And then, for just the briefest of moments, I saw the full form of a big dog fox, crossing my path directly ahead, his eyes still locked on mine, before he disappeared into the hedge. It is at moments like these, given a chance glimpse into the life of another species with whom we share this planet, that I feel shaken from my everyday existence. We live in worlds that are both parallel and yet shared. But rarely do we have the opportunity to meet their gaze. What, I wondered, must he have thought of me? Early mornings have always been my favourite time to run: they are a time to stumble upon the unexpected, and a time to simply *be*, moving through a world washed clean and refreshed by night, as yet unsullied by the stresses and strains of the day.

*

We had received several invitations to Christmas lunches with family and friends, but we decided we really wanted to spend it together in the tent. It felt like an important milestone to celebrate, surviving through to the darkest part of the year, our canvas home shining out into the darkness like the beacon of hope it had become to us. We would see our loved ones in the weeks after, but we chose for the day itself to be ours alone, surrounded by wild things, the trees and hills and the chatter of winter birds.

Christmas morning began like any other morning, with Sim braving the cold first to light the stove while I fed H. We stewed up apples with raisins, cinnamon and brown sugar and topped our porridge with it, sitting on cushions around the camping table, fairy lights sparkling overhead. Then we gave E her presents, delighting in her joy at finding the brightly wrapped packages that were all hers, watching her tear off the paper and discover the treasures within. H had a new toy, too, but he seemed to prefer the wrapping.

Lunch was a picnic of epic proportions. We had been shopping in nearby Wellington the day before and had bought all the things we usually looked at longingly but had to ration: fresh bread, smoked salmon, cheese, olives and more. We even shared a half bottle of Champagne, which made me pleasantly dizzy after more than a year without alcohol due to pregnancy and breastfeeding. It wasn't turkey and all the trimmings – it was so much better. That afternoon we explored together, wandering the empty lanes and following footpaths until we eventually made a full circle and arrived back at the tent for hot chocolate and Christmas cake, while H slept and E played with her new toys. We had decided not to buy anything for each other. Money was so short and simply enjoying the kids' excitement was more than enough. That, and the warm, happy knowledge that, unlike previous years, there was no looming return to the dragging normality of work once the festivities of Christmas and the New Year were over. For all its cold, dark, dampness, it was one of the warmest, brightest Christmases we had ever had.

While we had enjoyed the peace of such a different Christmas, as New Year approached, we were longing to see our families. Perhaps in an effort to frame this year as a challenge and an adventure, rather than simply a financial necessity, we still aimed to camp as much as we could. Whenever possible, we would pitch our backpacking tent in gardens, feeling the contrast as we stepped out into the cold darkness after warm evenings indoors.

We began our celebrations with my family in Bristol and the Midlands, enjoying reconnecting after a few weeks of struggling even to make regular phone calls. Although my sister is five years younger than me, we have always been close and talk or exchange messages on most days. She is the one person I know I can talk to about anything, without any fear of judgement. We have been through similar struggles in life – our parents' divorce, our rebellious teenage years, depressing jobs and even more depressing relationships – but have both found happiness in recent years. The strength of her bond with my children and, more recently, my bond with hers took us by surprise – but of course, it is not surprising: we are connected by something deeper than we know.

Seeing my family, it was as if a gap that had steadily opened up somewhere deep in my heart during our separation had been closed. I felt, as I always feel after even the briefest of visits to see them, a little more complete again. Leaving them to their respective New Year celebrations, we drove south to Dartmoor, pitching our backpacking tent in Sim's parents' front garden and spending the evenings with his family.

As each evening drew to a close, E and H growing either fractious or hyperactive with tiredness and overexcitement, we said our goodnights and left for the garden. It often felt like a wrench to leave, dragging ourselves away from the warmth of the fire and the comfort of the sofa. The tent was so cold and dark when we first clambered inside. And yet, once we were all tucked in under layers of down and wool, the heat from our bodies quickly mingling and warming our little space, there was no doubt at all that, more than anywhere else, this was where we were supposed to be.

Fragility
Restoration and repercussions in
Cornwall and the South Hams

WITH THE NEW YEAR came the first really cold nights of our trip. Heavy frosts iced the hedgerows and grass. Some mornings, we emerged from the tent to a world in which everything had grown long, delicate, blue-white feathers overnight. It was the most magical hoar frost we had ever seen, and E delighted in running her fingers along the hedgerows, watching the tiny ice crystals turn to a fine, cold dust as she went. The ground, now frozen hard, was wonderfully free from the mud that plagued us during the warmer, wetter spells. It was a joy to watch E embracing the freedom to roam around the fields to her heart's content, wrapped up in a bright red, padded all-in-one suit.

We had planned to spend a week or so wild camping on Dartmoor, but it was soon too cold to be comfortable. The owners of a basic campsite a few miles away were happy for us to stay and, with a whole field to ourselves, we would be able to pitch the Emperor and have the woodburner alight. We slept in our woolly hats but still, on some mornings, our faces glowed from the freezing overnight air. Yet, with the stove, our down duvets, many layers of clothing, including our full-length merino wool base layers, and our cosy bedroom tent we rarely actually felt cold. While we bathed E and H in the little tub by the fire, Sim and I braved the freezing cold showers only when absolutely necessary – there were many occasions when we (and probably those around us) were extremely grateful for wool's naturally antimicrobial properties.

Back in the wilds, after two weeks of being surrounded by people, we all fell ill. The kids and I caught flu and, although they recovered quickly, I continued to get worse. I developed mastitis, something that happened from time to time over the years I breastfed, and which usually wasn't too much of a problem, but which, this time, seemed to affect me much more in my already weakened state. Within a few days, I added tonsillitis and sinusitis to my growing list of woes, losing my voice and any desire to eat. My whole body ached and burned with infection.

I was loath to admit it, but it was so much harder being ill in the tent. I tried to simply soldier on but the woodsmoke from the stove scorched my sore throat, I was struggling to sleep through the cold nights and I just couldn't shake off the mastitis without antibiotics as I had done before. Concerned, Sim suggested we looked somewhere warm and dry for a few nights to allow me to recover.

'But we have to camp!' I protested weakly, furious with myself.

'Not if you're ill,' he said firmly. 'Let's find a cottage to rent for a week – we'll manage financially. You wouldn't hesitate if it was one of the kids. And anyway, we need you to be fixed.'

Hearing the tiredness in his voice – he'd had to take on much more than his fair share of everything, from childcare to the daily morning routine – I had to admit Sim was right. In my current state I was of little use to anyone.

After wrapping me up in every layer I had, we found a warm café for an internet connection and searched for somewhere suitable. Most places seemed to be closed for the winter, or full. Eventually, I found a farm just across the border into Cornwall that had availability for a week in one of its holiday cottages. I emailed them and had a reply straight back, which I read out to Sim.

'They've offered it to us for £200, which is cheap for what it is, but not actually cheap.' I said, ready, now the decision had been made for me, to take anything, just wanting to be warm, to be in a proper bed. 'What do you think?'

'Let's do it,' Sim replied, decisively. 'You'll have the best chance of getting well – and it sounds like it's in an awesome place so there'll be plenty for me and the kids to do.'

The little barn was basic and remote, but it felt like a palace to us, with a huge log burner that filled the place with glorious warmth. As soon as we got there, Sim took charge, insisting that I rested as much as possible. Usually, I find surrendering control to anyone else difficult – the idea of being helped and looked after bordering on unbearable – so it was a reflection of how bad I felt that I didn't resist relinquishing responsibility to Sim for a few days.

Cheerful and uncomplaining, he looked after us all, cooking, entertaining the kids and making me an endless supply of warm drinks as I could still barely eat. He took the children out exploring the surrounding fields and woods, often with H in the sling on his front and E riding high on his shoulders, giving me an hour or two to nap before they all piled back in with excited tales of boats and tractors and paddling in the stream in their wellies.

After a few days of rest, warm dry air, hot baths and a comfortable bed I felt well enough to start gently exploring the local coastline with them – the excitement that I felt welling up inside me at the prospect of being outside again a sure sign I was on the mend. And I could feel the gradual rise of that familiar yearning: to escape the stuffiness of indoor life; to wake each morning to cold air and birdsong, to strip back the clutter and convenience of everyday life and return to the simplicity of our life under canvas. The break had done its job. Now, it was time to get back to the tent.

*

To see the last of winter through to spring, we had managed to secure a five-week pitch on a farm in the South Hams Area of Outstanding Natural Beauty, the peninsula that reaches southwards from Dartmoor to the sea. At £10 per night including water, electric hook-up and use of washrooms usually reserved for glampers over the summer months, it sounded perfect. We packed the truck and said goodbye to the little corner of Cornwall that had offered us such a necessary retreat for the past week, then made our way east along the coast and back over the border into Devon.

Winding down narrow, hedge-lined lanes towards the sea I was excited, all over again, about the weeks ahead. And this time, having learnt our lesson about coastal storm winds and tents back in November, we had a new tactic. We had decided to leave the bell tent and stove at Sim's parents' house, and instead pack an old but well-cared for family tent – a Mountain Hardwear Casa – which we would use alongside our backpacking tent. With electricity on-tap, we wouldn't need the stove for heating, and it felt easier and safer to set up a sheltered cooking area outside the tent. H was now crawling and could move with alarming speed, particularly the moment we took our eyes of him. Unlike E, however, he was not yet old enough to understand the dangers of venturing near the stove. Having it alight in the tent now required constant vigilance to the point where it was impossible to get anything else done. So, although it gave us considerably less space, using this more traditional family tent, made from a double skin of polyester with an aerodynamic design rather than the sail-like cotton canvas of the bell tent, seemed to make a lot of sense. I also loved the translation of the Spanish word, *casa*: home.

We pulled up in a rambling farmyard to be met by a cheerful woman with wiry grey hair, warmly welcoming and enthusiastic about our adventure. I was always so heartened when people were positive and encouraging about our plans. Even though I had no doubts myself, it always rattled me to be met with accusations of craziness.

As we walked towards a small field edged by rough hedges and thick gorse, our friendly host asked us about our year, seeming genuinely interested and caring. I thought about the many ways in which those with whom we had stayed over the last few months, or made arrangements for those to come, had shaped our experiences – the importance of that human connection. Overwhelmingly, people had been incredibly kind, welcoming and helpful. The generosity of the campsite owners, farmers and smallholders who had offered us places to stay throughout the year had made it not just possible, but even more meaningful.

'Take care.' She smiled as she left us to settle in. 'I'll pop back now and again to check you're all OK. Give me a shout if you need anything.' And then she was off, striding away up the field in her wellies.

Beyond the hedge, cows and sheep grazed the exposed coastal grasslands and, beyond them, the glittering blue of the sea stretched away to the horizon. On that breezy, sunny afternoon, the whole picture of land and sea and sky was a palette of dazzling greens and blues. We pitched both the Casa and our backpacking tent, tucked into the most sheltered corner of the field, giving us a bright, roomy space for our days and a snug, cosy one for our nights.

That evening, spreading out OS Explorer map OL20 (South Devon, Brixham to Newton Ferrers) on the tent floor, we traced the South West Coast Path to the east and west by the light of our headtorches, finding the numerous beaches and coves nearby that we were all keen to explore. I pointed out the names of the headlands, coves and islands off this stretch of the coast to E, enjoying their names, which told of adventure and history: Great Mew Stone, Blackstone Point, Butcher's Cove, Ivy Island, Hoist Beach, Gutterslide Beach, Mary's Rocks, Beacon Point and Burgh Island – famous for its Art Deco hotel, where Agatha Christie wrote two of her detective novels. Looking at the hotel's rates out of sheer nosiness, I discovered we could spend three nights in Agatha's Beach House for about the same money as we had budgeted on accommodation for the entire year.

That first morning in our South Hams field, we awoke to bright sunshine, already starting to melt the feathery ice that crusted the grass, hedgerows and a thin layer on the outside of our tent. We also now had a new routine. Without the stove to light, breakfast was so much quicker to prepare. First moving the heater from the backpacking tent into the Casa to warm up the air ready for breakfast time, then following with the kids, wrapped up warm in blankets. Porridge bubbled away on the double burner in front of the tent, while water for coffee heated in a Jetboil – a super-efficient, insulated, integrated stove, perfectly designed for making hot drinks in cold places. Our water now heated up so quickly that we challenged ourselves to race it with the coffee grinder, furiously turning the handle to grind enough coffee before the water boiled.

After breakfast, once the sun had risen far enough in the sky to warm the air to above freezing, we packed rucksacks with enough provisions to see us through many hours of wandering: food, blankets, spare clothes, buckets and spades and our Kelly Kettle. From the farm, a track led down the gently sloping hillside to the coast path, then along a narrow tunnel through a dense tangle of shrubbery, descending a steep slope to a cove. Emerging from the undergrowth, we walked out onto a perfect crescent of pale, unmarked sand. Bordered by rocky outcrops, it was completely sheltered from the wind that had been a constant companion higher up.

We spent a while ambling about, familiarising ourselves with the finer details of the cove. At first it seemed deserted but, as we explored, finding sandy patches, narrow caves, boulder stacks and hidden rockpools, we began to notice how much life existed in this hidden place. Gulls circled overhead, their mewing calls filling the air, or landed on nearby rocks to watch us with keen, greedy eyes. Red-legged oystercatchers and huddles of turnstones, barely visible in their brindle camouflage, scratched about searching the pebbles at one end of the beach. Gannets soared, folded and dropped like darts into the waves. Snakelocks and beadlet anemones waved colourful fronds in the clear water of limpet-clad rockpools.

As we went, we gathered dry wood for the Kelly Kettle, then building a small fire in the base and placing the main metal container filled with water on top to boil. E kept herself busy collecting fresh wood to keep the fire burning. I often thought of this tough, double-walled heater as more than a just kettle – more than warm drinks to fuel an adventure. Using it *was* an adventure.

Over the days, and then weeks that followed we gradually came to know the coastline within walking distance of our tent. The furthest-away beach was E's favourite: a vast expanse of wave-sculpted sand, awaiting her bucket and spade. She and Sim spent one whole morning making a long, curving line of sandcastles running from the water's edge all the way to the fine, dry sand where I sat with H. When they were finished, we sat back and watched the sea claim each one in turn as the tide came in. Even the fact that it was an hour-long walk each way didn't stop E asking to go to this particular beach most days.

Those weeks in the South Hams coincided with some of the best of the winter weather. Though it was often cold and windy, especially overnight, daytimes were clear and sunny and often surprisingly warm. High on the parallel headland to the one we were camping on, reached by following the South West Coast Path into a steep-sided valley and back out again, stood a large rock that soon became a favourite place: a sun-warmed shelter commanding a grand view of the bay, with the surrounding coastline and countryside stretching away to either side. From this secret lookout, we watched a peregrine hunting around the cliffs, buzzards circling over the fields and flocks of cirl buntings busily flitting between the scraggy hedges and bare trees. Sometimes a seal broke the surface of the water, its dark, round head glistening in the sun. Gulls screamed and swooped. Once a fox, trotting along a nearby path, stopped, looked, sniffed the air, then continued on its way. Even in the depths of winter, this place, far from any people other than a few scattered farms and cottages, was vibrant and alive.

Thinking back to that time, it is the warmth of the winter sun, the soothingly rhythmic wash of the sea, the steeply rolling bright green fields that run right up to the edge of the land and the feeling of endless, unhurried time for exploration that I remember. And yet my diary also reminds me that the weather wasn't always kind. Twice, fierce storms battered our tent overnight: hail and wind, blackness and fury, the thunder of the waves huge and violent against the coastline below. Snug in our backpacking tent, we didn't fear the storms at all, but we could hear the larger Casa, next to us, flapping and billowing in the wind. Each morning, though, it was still standing, unscathed by the battering.

'Do you think we made a mistake buying the Emperor?' Sim was checking our tents over after a particularly windy night, while I made coffee. 'I don't think it would have coped well with this.'

I looked at our friendly pair of tents, nestled companionably beneath the hedge. I thought about the ease of pitching them, how well they shrugged off the onslaught of the wind.

'Maybe . . .' I had been thinking the same for some time without admitting it – even to myself. Knowing I would never entirely trust the big tent again in bad weather, which realistically wrote off camping in the UK at any time of the year. 'I love living in a bell tent though. It's sad if we just give up on it.'

There were many plus points for bell tents in general – they're simple, hardwearing, incredibly waterproof and, with their natural cotton canvas allowing plenty of light and fresh air in, a joy to live in, especially over the warm summer months. But, in trying to allow ourselves enough space to live comfortably for so many months, had we gone too big? We didn't need to make a decision right away – we had plenty of space for both tents in our little field – but, at some point, a double pitch would be too expensive and we would have to choose.

*

Slowing down, living life at the pace of young children, our days and nights structured around the rhythms of the natural world, we were learning – relearning – to notice. I no longer felt like a passenger in my own life – out of control, barely able to focus on the world around me as it flashed by, day after busy day. Instead, I was now deeply within that world, noticing and absorbing its subtleties and textures. For the kids, each new stage of their development showed them the world as completely new. As their ability to comprehend, to draw on previous experiences, to control their motor skills and interpret their sensory ones grew, their perception of the world and everything in it shifted constantly.

The previous winter, back in our house in the Cotswolds, E had been just two. In the year since, her ability to observe, comprehend and communicate her observations had grown exponentially. H, at his own stage of development, was reaching, touching, tasting – engaging more with us and his surroundings every day. We watched them as, each in their own way, they experienced the sensations of frost and ice on warm fingers, of sand and seawater on bare feet, of wind and rain on the soft skin of their faces. These things were all so normal a part of every passing winter for us that we almost become numb to them. But now we found ourselves reliving and re-experiencing these sensations, guided by our children. We hoped, in turn, that by raising our children surrounded by the fascinating, precious and irreplaceable natural world, it wouldn't just be something they appreciated and enjoyed – it would become part of their souls.

The year was teaching us to slow down in other ways, too. Before we had moved into the tent, I had wondered whether I would find the lack of convenience difficult, especially with two such young children to look after. On campsites, where we were usually pitched well out of the way in our big tent, it was often a long walk to the toilet block, washing-up sinks or the water tap with containers to refill. Cooking was rarely simple and never quick. But we were finding a joy in these simple acts of daily existence. Instead of being rushed through as they had been before, when we had worked long hours apart to keep all the conveniences to which we had become accustomed, and therefore never questioned, around us, these daily routines and rituals – our quotidian – felt newly and freshly important. As if each one was an essential part of a fulfilling whole and therefore worth the time and care it took to do well. Thoreau observed that 'wealth is the ability to fully experience life' and we were certainly finding that this complete immersion in every aspect of life was making it so much richer.

*

For weeks, E had been talking about snow. Friends further north had sent photos of their children building snowmen, throwing snowballs, sledging and making snow angels. On a few occasions, away in the distance, we had spotted a light dusting like icing sugar across the tops of the high moor. But here, next to the sea, we'd had none at all.

Then, one evening, we heard there had been a good fall of snow at Princetown on the highest part of Dartmoor, with more forecast overnight. We set out early the next morning, aiming for the tall mast that stands above the village, a prominent landmark visible across much of Dartmoor. As we steadily gained height, the patches of snow on the verges grew in size along with E's excitement.

It felt bitingly cold when we stepped out of the truck, and we fumbled in our haste to zip up padded all-in-one suits and fiddle tiny, bendy fingers through the impossible maze of gloves. But finally we were all ready and we set out, H in his sling and E running on ahead, laughing, sliding and falling over in the snow as we walked out on the main track towards the first granite-topped hill on the horizon. Our aim was to spend a couple of hours walking and exploring, then find a café to warm up in.

After less than half an hour, E was already tired, cold and miserable. H began screaming from his sling, the tiny part of his face that was exposed to the elements turning blotchy and purple with rage. We looked at each other, then at the bleak, open moorland that offered nothing in the way of shelter, feeling a mixture of irritation and guilt. As noisy chaos began to take hold, we made the decision to stop and turn around.

Back in Princetown, we dived into the Fox Tor café, a place we hadn't been since our pre-child days, and sat together by an open fire with mugs of hot chocolate, warming cold fingers and toes.

An hour later we tried again. The moor seemed like a different place altogether. We walked further than we had planned. E ran around, keeping herself warm, cheerfully making tracks and snow angels. H was at first fascinated by it all and then fell into a deep slumber against my chest. In the end, after initially getting it so wrong, we realised we had made two good calls: first in admitting defeat and beating a hasty retreat, and second, getting back out and having another go. The fine art of knowing when to push on and when to give up and turn around was something we were learning as each day passed.

*

If we had been living in a house, it would have been barely noticeable. But for us now, living so much outdoors, the gradual lengthening of the days as January gave way to February was already evident, and exciting. At 5 p.m., as we cooked supper under the tarp outside the tent, we could still clearly see the long blue glimmer of the sea, luminous and streaked with silver beneath a low winter sun. The mornings were still incredibly dark, though. The same view at 6.30 a.m., as I put water on to boil, was a sea of unsettling blackness dotted with boats: tiny caterpillars of glowing lights.

For all its bleakness, I have a fondness for February. It is, in many ways, a time of celebration, not least because it means January is done. But also, like pinpricks of excitement dotted throughout the month, are causes for celebration. Valentine's day; pancake day. The day when the first snowdrops open their tiny, delicate white and green flowers. And, later on, the first daffodils and primroses filling the woods and verges of the south-west with sunshine. Blooming into the cold, dark winter days, these flowers always feel like a triumph of light over dark, a promise of all the light and warmth and life that will emerge over the coming weeks. And this year, even more than usual. The final week of February, which always feels like a step over winter's threshold into spring, is also my birthday.

The meaning of these celebrations became even more important now that we were no longer surrounded by the incessant shouting of consumerism. We needed these days, set apart from all the other days, special, separate from the steady passage of time. Each held an essence, all of its own, and we would shape the day around this, drawing from old traditions and creating new ones, making them ours. E loved making tiny, hand-drawn cards for us all for Valentine's, and we made our own for each other, too. We cooked hot, heart-shaped drop-scones on the stove for breakfast, piling them with strawberry jam and clotted cream from the local farm shop. It was messy, and the heart shapes were rather approximate, but it was a perfect way to begin the day.

I had always avoided what I considered to be the mass over-commercialisation of Valentine's day before, but this year it felt like a celebration purely of love – love for each other, for those we missed, for this way of life and for the fragile and precious world around us. For the essential delicate facets of trust and respect and the power of togetherness.

Three days later, pancake day was less successful. We had recently agreed to test out a new stove for a company, an ingenious device which could both burn any small pieces of solid fuel and use the energy to drive a tiny turbine that would generate enough electricity to charge our phones.

It was a beautiful morning, cold, clear and crisp, so we decided to cook our pancakes outside in the morning sun, using the new stove. Sim and the kids set out to find small sticks as fuel to keep the fire burning, while I got it going with some dry kindling from the wood pile. I had mixed up a basic batter and, when the stove was burning well and the little fan whirring, I added some oil to a frying pan on the top. As the oil began to heat, I poured in some batter and swirled it gently to coat the base of the pan, then left it to cook through and start to crisp up around the edges. Meanwhile, E kept herself busy feeding in new wood to keep the fire going and for a few minutes it all looked as if it was going to work.

Unfortunately, not all of the new wood was completely dry and, combined with the freezing cold morning air, this cooled the fire until it was a smoking pile of ash and the pancake stopped cooking. We carefully got the fire going again, set the pan back on top and tried again. But once more the fire went out before the pancake was cooked. In the end, I was left with a rubbery heap of warmed-through batter, far from the hot stack of crispy, maple syrup-drenched joy I had imagined. Disconsolately, I scraped it into the bin, lamenting the pointless waste of eggs. By this time everyone was ravenous and I was grumpy, so we all ate cereal and promised to have a go at pancakes the following day, after replenishing our supplies of milk and eggs at the farm shop. Freed from the hefty expectations of Shrove Tuesday, those pancakes, of course, turned out perfectly.

*

As the light slowly returned, so too did our desire for new adventures. Our year planner was starting to fill up with deadlines for writing and photography commissions, invitations to talk at festivals and bookshops and meetings with publishers. We were keen to start writing a second guidebook, this time one that encouraged families to get out exploring and had approached some publishers with our idea. If we could secure another book deal, the money from the advance would be a huge help to our budget.

For the moment, though, money was incredibly tight. I had started struggling to sleep again, something I hadn't suffered so far on our trip, spending long nights lying in the darkness wondering how we were going to make it through the weeks and months ahead. What if none of the publishers liked our idea? Without a new book, would the rest of our work also dry up?

As we approached the final week of our stay in the South Hams our thoughts began to turn to packing away and moving on once more. Perhaps made worse by the unsettling necessity of leaving what had become a such special place to us over the past weeks, that familiar weighty anxiety over our finances was almost suffocating. It was very early one morning and I had been lying awake for hours, worry coursing through me like electricity. Up until now we had been just about managing to make our meagre income stretch to cover our food, camping, fuel and our debt repayments but, unless something changed – and fast – we would soon be back in real difficulty. Without our debts, our income from tax credits and work would easily cover our outgoings, but with the hefty repayments we were making, I couldn't see how we were going to get through the next few weeks.

Eventually, I resigned myself to the fact that there would be no more sleep that night. Once H had finished his first feed of the day and fallen into a deep, milk-induced slumber, I slid out of the warmth of the bed and, already half-dressed, added a few more layers, plus a headtorch, armouring myself against the February morning outside.

'I can't sleep so I'm going to head out for a run,' I told Sim, leaning over to his side of the bed in the darkness to kiss him goodbye. 'I won't be more than a couple of hours, so hopefully H will sleep through.'

Sim hugged me with his warm, powerful arms; they always make everything better.

'You go and have an awesome run. We'll all be totally fine.'

I knew this, of course. But my guilt at leaving was so strong in those early years. I knew, too, that Sim understood my need to run, to use movement as a means of detangling the mess of anxious threads that filled my mind. Sometimes I came back to find they had not been fine; that one or both children had spent the past hour crying unconsolably. Sometimes I would cry my own tears as I ran, the wind whipping them across my face as I forced myself forward; forced myself to increase the distance between myself and my family in order to return to them happier and stronger. But I always knew that with Sim to look after them, E and H would be more than just *fine* – they would be flourishing.

When I returned to my family on that bright February morning, I had run through a spectacular sunrise that had painted the hills with rose and gold. Following the rising and falling coastal trails, I felt soothed by the restless waves, comforted by the rhythm of my run, easing and loosening the tightness of my worries and setting them free to fly away on the sea wind. I unzipped the door to find E and H happily playing with their books and blocks and the tent fresh and spotless. Sim had swept, cleaned and tidied our little home. A clean cloth was spread over our camping table and coffee and porridge was ready on the stove. The tears, this time, were of pure gratitude.

But for all the good it did me, that sunrise run had not solved any of our money worries. I couldn't keep spending my nights awake – my worrying wasn't solving anything. We needed help. Later that day, I walked across the field and rang a debt helpline, standing in the shelter of the hedge furthest from the sea so I could hear and be heard, above the wind. The advisor's voice was cool and detached, her manner clipped and efficient. I read out the details of our income and expenditure from the list I'd made. I could hear her typing, then there was a pause.

'Your expenditure is very low,' she commented finally. 'I'm not sure how it's possible for you to live on so little.'

'We live in a tent,' I said.

Another pause. More typing. Then she spoke again.

'We need to be realistic. We need to include a realistic amount of expenditure for a family of four. You don't have enough money coming in to cover these and your credit card repayments.'

'No – I know.' Tears were pricking at my eyes again. 'But we're . . . we're really trying.' I knew that, right at that moment, all our efforts were meaningless: they didn't matter in the slightest. That trying, evidently, had not been good enough, which was why I was on the phone. But I didn't know what else to say.

'Have you considered bankruptcy?'

This time the silence was mine. Bankruptcy? The word cut into me. Cold and hard and heavy with failure. We had tried so hard, given up so much, lived on so little, kept up our repayments for so long. How had it come to this?

We could, she continued, either wait for our creditors to take action against us or take matters into our own hands and petition for our own bankruptcy. This latter option would cost us precious funds but would be quicker and far easier given our precarious living arrangements. I took down the details the advisor gave me about how to petition for bankruptcy and hung up. Then, feeling sick and a little shaky, I walked slowly back to the tent to speak to Sim.

He was characteristically optimistic – at least we would be making the decision ourselves, rather than giving up and letting it happen to us. We had nothing of our own to lose: no house, no savings, no possessions of any value apart from the truck, the laptop and the camera. And, as we needed these for work, it was likely we would be allowed to keep them. Once everything was settled, the advisor had told me, we would be free of the debts that were making our lives so difficult. Yes, we had got ourselves into this position, using our credit cards to pay for groceries. But at the time it had been that or nothing. We had paid so much back in interest already, it was hard to imagine our creditors were losing out too much, but still the idea of simply cancelling our debts didn't sit well. We could only hope that, without the monthly repayments, we could really begin to work ourselves into a place of, at least relative, financial stability.

At the time, it sounded as though the process of declaring ourselves bankrupt would be fairly straightforward. We would need to close our existing bank account and open a new one, without any 'benefits' in the form of overdrafts or credit cards. We should inform our creditors that the debts were no longer our responsibility and refer them to the Official Receiver at the court. And we would not be allowed to borrow more than £500 or work as company directors or Insolvency Practitioners for up to a year. Other than that, we were told, we were free to carry on as before.

The reality, we would discover, turned out to be somewhat more complicated.

We visited a nearby court, filling in lengthy forms and handing over a wadge of cash to pay for our individual petitions. Bankruptcy, ironically, isn't cheap. Back then, it cost us £525 each; at the time of writing, in England and Wales, it's £680. We had no money, other than what we needed immediately to live on, so our only option was to withdraw all the remaining balances left on our credit cards to pay for our bankruptcy petitions. It seemed ridiculous but we were out of other options. At least, once this was all over, money would be a little easier.

With only a few days left in the South Hams, after so many uplifting experiences and incredible days spent on the beaches and coast path, I felt crushed, now, by this turn of events. Our whole adventure had been planned around restoring and improving our financial situation, avoiding the intervention of authorities, claiming our freedom, making it on our own and in our own way. And now we had a court case to get through, questions about our life to answer, judgements to face. I looked out at the sea – flat, grey and sombre beneath a steel grey sky, perfectly reflecting my mood.

*

On our last evening in the South Hams, everything packed and ready except our bedroom tent and what we needed to sleep in, I reflected on a time of highs and lows: the joy of being surrounded by the vastness of the rolling blue–green coastal landscape. Watching the endless interplay of sea and sun and sky from the tent door. The warmth of winter sun, and long days at the beach. We had flourished in this corner of Devon, with its mild weather and endless things to do within an easy, safe walk. This was a place filled with adventurous treasure for curious children, and it had enchanted us, too.

We were sobered by our financial struggles, however, and this unexpected unpleasant ending. But still, returning to the tent after chores in the cold darkness that evening, stepping through the door onto a scene of warmth, light, laughter and love, I could only be glad and grateful that we were here.

We needed to return to Dartmoor for a few days to await the letter that would give us the date and time for our court hearing. Sim and I were subdued and talked little as we followed the winding, steeply climbing lanes. Living this way had not, as we had hoped, immediately solved our financial woes. And yet, despite ourselves, we found our moods lifting as the moorland landscape opened out around us. E chattered away in the back, already filled with excitement about seeing her grandparents, visiting her favourite places and finding friendly Dartmoor ponies. Her enthusiasm was contagious and soon we were joining in, planning adventures for these few extra days on the moor.

*

A week later we walked into the court together, unaccustomed to our smart, clean shoes which squeaked on the polished wooden floor. We were ready to face the judgement we knew awaited us, but desperate for freedom from the debts that had weighed so heavily on us for so long. In the end, because the amounts we owed were relatively small, although still insurmountable in relation to our tiny income, our petitions were simply granted without the need to be seen by anyone other than the clerk. I had even prepared a defence in my head: the loss of my income; the lack of maternity pay; the high cost of renting; and the monumental effort we had put into trying to live more cheaply. But in the end I needed none of these excuses. We were free to go and it was time to move on.

SPRING

'There is symbolic as well as actual beauty in the migration of birds, the ebb and flow of the tides, the folded bud ready for the spring. There is something infinitely healing in the repeated refrains of nature – the assurance that dawn comes after night, and spring after the winter.'

Rachel Carson, *The Sense of Wonder.*

Gratitude

The kindness of strangers in Dorset and on Exmoor

THE DAY WE ARRIVED in Lyme Regis, we had driven from Dartmoor, via a doctor's surgery in Exeter, where we had booked E in to have her pre-school vaccinations. She had never been keen on doctors, but I buried my concerns about how it was all going to go beneath a front of cheerful positivity. I have no doubts about the efficacy of vaccinations, but it's still hard to watch a stranger inflict pain on your child. It had all started well. I had talked to E about what would happen, and why it was important, and she had agreed to go. We left Sim and H waiting in the car park and made our way through to the waiting room, E relaxed and happy, taking in everything about these strange new sights, sounds and smells. I began to wonder whether my fears had been entirely unfounded.

We were called in and sat for a few minutes, chatting with two friendly nurses, who asked E about her favourite cartoon characters. Then, without warning, they stealthily produced a needle each and simultaneously plunged them into both of her tiny arms. For a brief moment E looked at me in shocked silence, wide eyed, disbelieving. I had not only allowed this happen to her but convinced her it was a good idea!

Then she started screaming.

'All done!' announced one of the nurses, a little too cheerfully. 'Calpol!'

'Sticker?' said the other.

I picked E up, and thanked the two women, for whom I felt at once desperately sorry, incredibly grateful, and, somewhere deep within my feral maternal heart, an instinct to bite. I left with the still-screaming E in my arms, hurrying past the kids and their mums waiting patiently in the seating area for their turn.

The Calpol was violently rejected, covering the back of the truck in sticky pink goo. Cuddles, soothing words and even chocolate buttons did nothing to help, so we set off for Dorset, with E still inconsolable, hoping that at some point she would wear herself out.

By the time we reached Lyme Regis, E and H had fallen asleep and the rain was bucketing down. If we could, we tried to avoid actually pitching the tent while it was raining. It was hard enough to keep the inside of the tent clean and dry at the best of times; getting everything soaked in transit from the truck to the tent was not a good way to begin. On that grey afternoon, we stopped in the car park on Lyme Regis seafront and sat looking out at the grey sea, the grey sky and the grey harbour wall in front of us in companionable, exhausted silence.

The rain on the outside, and the fog from our breath on the inside, gradually blurred, then obscured, our view through the windows. I found this slow loss of definition oddly comforting, softening the still-sharp memories of the morning. It felt good to have finally stopped, too, and to know we had a pitch waiting for us only a couple of miles up the road. But we were both too shattered to contemplate setting up camp yet. Finally, after nearly two hours, stiff, hungry and desperate for fresh air, I ran through sideways sheets of rain to the nearest takeaway and bought chips for us all. By the time I got back to the truck, the kids were awake and sitting with Sim in the front, E happy and pretending to drive, the trauma of the morning forgotten.

*

Later, when the rain cleared, we made our way along the slippery, wet stones on top of the Cobb, each of us holding one of E's hands tightly in ours. This curved stone harbour wall always seems more sculpture than building, mirroring the arc of the bay – or perhaps that of an ammonite shell. It has captured the imaginations of many over the years, and appears in both Jane Austen's *Persuasion* and John Fowles' *The French Lieutenant's Woman*. Fowles was inspired to write his novel by the image of a woman standing on the Cobb, staring out to sea, and lived for a while in a remote farmhouse overlooking the bay.

A persistent breeze gusted in off the sea, pushing at us as we walked. Big waves broke on the wall below, showering us with salty spray. It was exciting, exhilarating, almost as if we were walking over the top of the waves, all the way to Victoria Pier at the far end. From there the view of the Jurassic Coast was spectacular. It was a view of the land from out at sea, stretching from the colourful seafront at Lyme Regis eastwards to the pebble bay at Charmouth; the green stone-topped pinnacle of Golden Cap – the highest point on the south coast of England; the long, grey line of Chesil Beach; and finally to Portland Bill, the last visible point of land before the emptiness of open water.

*

Our campsite was in Uplyme, a tiny village which, as its name suggests, lies upstream from Lyme Regis. Peaceful, welcoming and surrounded by steep-sided hills and hidden valleys, it felt like an ideal spot to spend the next three weeks, at a very generously discounted £5 per night. We had decided to take The Emperor, knowing from previous visits that the site was sheltered and had plenty of space. We had bought a cheap fireguard – a folding fence which we set up around the stove to deter H in his crawling explorations of the tent. This seemed to work well and doubled brilliantly as a place to hang our wet waterproofs. It also divided up the tent so that we could now *almost* imagine we had a separate kitchen, living room and bedroom.

It was a pretty walk of a couple of miles following the course of the River Lym from the campsite down through fields and quiet lanes to reach the sea, a voyage we made often. One particularly beautiful spring day, we continued westwards along the South West Coast Path, discovering the mysterious and inescapable

Undercliff. Linking Lyme Regis with Axmouth, this seven-mile section of the coast path is a dynamic, changeable ecosystem, where landslips continually recreate a sealed-off wilderness, colonised by a fantastic abundance of life.

That day, we wandered through a wild woodland of ash and field maple, through scrubby clearings of bright pink berried spindle, honey-scented wayfaring trees – named for their habit of growing alongside paths – dense entanglements of bramble, and wild clematis. E pointed out some round, black objects growing on branches – King Alfred's cakes, also known as coal fungus. Sunny yellow primroses and wild daffodils patterned the woodland floor. Now and then, where there was a break in the dense foliage, we could see the sea sparkling up at us from below. Years ago, I had read about this place in my parents' copy of Elaine Franks' 1989 book, *The Undercliff: a Naturalist's Sketchbook of the Devon to Dorset Coast,* finding myself utterly entranced by the author's intricate sketches and paintings and vivid descriptions of the terrain, wildlife and weather. At the time I had imagined what it would feel like to feel to be there – its smells and textures, light and sound. And now, having experienced it not just through my own senses but those of my children, it was even more glorious than I had always hoped it would be.

*

While weekdays were still quiet, weekends at the campsite were slowly starting to get busier. On Friday evenings, as we ate supper together, couples and families began arriving in smart, clean campervans, always, I felt, looking a world away from our well-worn, weathered muddiness.

Later on in the evenings we would hear the distinctive slide and slam of VW campervan doors – a bedtime chorus – as other families settled in for the night. Only very occasionally, as I walked past on my way to the washing up sinks, did a small part of me long for that ability to shut the noisy, windy, rainy world out. But for the most part, I knew I needed the richness we gained by sleeping against the earth, the immersive wonder of living so much within the unceasing flow of the outdoors. For the time being, this was still the challenge I craved – the raw, tough, unrelenting challenge that was simply getting through each day, each week and each month – a process through which I felt myself growing stronger and more sure of myself as each day passed.

I wasn't sure how I felt about the peaceful, empty fields we had spent the past months enjoying the full run of filling up with other campers. E, though, has always been very sociable and loved it when there were other children about to make friends with. That weekend, she spent Saturday morning playing with two girls of around her age who had arrived in a campervan the night before. Sim was out for the day, running and photographing a nearby route for a magazine article. I wandered about with H, who could now toddle short distances if I held both his hands, keeping half an eye on E and her new friends. It was approaching lunchtime, so we made our way over to see if E was hungry and found the girls' mum handing out packets of sweets and smoothies in cartons. The expression on E's face was one of ecstasy, as she held out her hands to receive the unaccustomed bounty. The mum looked up as I approached.

'I hope it's OK for her to have these.' She smiled benevolently.
'Yes – of course!'

I wasn't sure what else to say. I didn't mind particularly.
E rarely ate sweets and was so clearly delighted. 'Thank you
very much. E – did you say thank you?' E mumbled something
through a mouthful.

The mum and I chatted for a while, exchanging covert
glances – me at her expensive haircut, spotless leather boots and
manicured nails, and her, presumably in horror, at my battered
old Buffalo jacket, beanie hat and faded jeans that were wearing
through at the knees. The sliding door of their van was open to
reveal a scene of colour-co-ordinated perfection. I thought of the
patchwork homeliness of our tent, the love I had for our rusty
old truck and the freedom to stay or go that I so treasured. In
that moment, I wouldn't have given up our way of life for all the
campervans in Dorset.

*

Popular to the point of bursting over the summer months, in the
chilly quiet of the off-season, Lyme Regis beach was like a glorious
secret. The beaches nearest to the Cobb were remodelled in the
early 2000s, using fine, pale sand imported from France, shingle
from the Isle of Wight and Larvikite boulders from Norway, to
stabilise the coast and protect the homes and businesses along
the seafront. It was perfect for the kids, who had the luxury of
being able to choose sand or pebbles, right next to each other.

Further along the coastline, towards Charmouth, is fossil
country, where a morning spent ambling about aimlessly,

pushing stones about with our hands, invariably unearthed some fascinating finds, including curled ammonites and straight, squid-like belemnites. The best ammonite we spotted hung tantalisingly high up a crumbling cliff face: huge, perfect, ancient and yet, surely, destined to break into a thousand fragments on the rocks below with the next shift of the land.

Having the coast so close once more felt like an opportunity we should embrace as often as possible. So, on dry days, we walked the two miles downstream to the beach, spending the morning sitting on the rounded pebbles above the sand or paddling in the shallows.

These were rare moments of something approaching relaxation, when Sim and I could simply sit together for a while, absented from the need to do chores or provide entertainment. E and H played close by, while we shared a flask of coffee and talked about work – from what was approaching its deadline to ideas for future projects. I was surprised at how much work we were able to get done, sharing childcare and the time consuming but necessary chores of daily life. I found a new sense of clarity and direction, sitting on a cushion on the tent floor with my laptop on one of our sturdy packing boxes, that I hadn't felt before. Even having the kids playing nearby, as long as Sim was with them, was never too much of a distraction. Thinking back to my days in our rented house in the Cotswolds, I remembered the total lack of time and space for writing – and the frustration and guilt of trying to carve even the tiniest of gaps into our days.

Back on the beach, H played with the large, round pebbles which, unlike the smaller stones he sought out at many campsites, were too big for him to consider putting in his mouth. E loved paddling at the water's edge, squealing with the cold at first, but soon happy to let the waves wash over her feet. One morning, as she was scooping up seaweed and pebbles with her long-handled net, we heard her exclaim in delight.

'Look Mummy and Daddy!' she was running over to where we sat, holding the contents of the net out to show us. 'They're . . . MOVING!'

We peered in quizzically. Huddled in the bottom of the net was an assortment of twisted shells which, as we watched, began to twitch, and then move more definitely. Tiny claws emerged, feeling their way out and then faces with dark, beady eyes and long antennae. It was our first experience of hermit crabs, and completely magical. We all watched them with utter fascination before E returned them carefully to the sea. Later, we read about them, showing E how they line up in size order, each one waiting for a new home that's a perfect fit.

Sometimes, on our walk down to the sea, we bought warm croissants from a lovely bakery where we could sit on long benches surrounded by a warm buzz of friendly chatter. More often though, we told E, 'Not today.' Funds were still very tight. One afternoon, as we were passing by on our way back to the tent, I saw a woman from the bakery standing in the doorway and smiled, recognising her from our visits.

'Oh wait, stop a minute!' she called as we were about to walk on. 'Do you want to take anything? We're closing and there's loads left over.' We were all ravenous and had been planning to cook supper the moment we reached the tent. But E was already fractious, wanting to be carried, repeatedly requesting food, only we had used up all our supplies on the beach and now had none with us. We instantly and enthusiastically accepted the offer and made our way over.

We had chatted with this kind lady a few times before, and she had been interested in our adventures. She must, too, have guessed why we didn't often call by for breakfast. I had to fight back the tears as she piled pizza and croissants into bags for us to take with us, refusing to accept any payment.

'Are you really sure this is OK?' I asked, hoping she understood how much the gesture meant to us. Our eyes met and I knew she knew.

'Honestly – it's more than OK.' She still held my gaze, pressing the paper bags firmly into my hands. 'It's my pleasure.'

We thanked her, several times over, and she waved us on our way, E perched on Sim's shoulders, already tucking in. Supper that night was a random but delightful assortment.

*

At 191 metres above sea level, the summit of Golden Cap is the highest point on the south coast of England. Seeing it from the end of the Cobb, on that first grey morning in Lyme Regis, I had felt drawn to its conical peak, the golden summit that gives the hill its name, and we had decided to walk it as soon as the weather allowed.

We set out on a beautiful morning, sunshine filtering through the trees, flickering the path ahead of us. The walking was easy to start, contouring Langdon Hill on a wide, sweeping track edged with beech, birch, hazel and Scots pine. The air smelled of damp wood and moss, sweet, sharp pine and a hint of salt from the sea, which lay out of sight somewhere over the other side of the hill. E ran ahead, showing us the way, peering into every hole in every log, veering off onto tiny tracks that vanished into the woods then jumping out as we approached.

Rounding a corner, our eyes met those of two roe deer standing motionless on the path ahead. We stopped, locked in their gaze. Even the children were quiet, held captive in the moment, the only sounds the bright chirrup of birds and the soft sigh of the wind in the trees around us. And then they were off, all legs and white tails, crashing through the woodland, vanishing from our sight. Just as suddenly, we were released from their spell, carrying on with our walk, laughing and chatting as if we had stepped out of, and then back into, time.

Emerging from the woods, a curving, sloping, landscape of bright grassy hills edged by sea and sky opened out before us. Tufts of trees stood out here and there, dark and wiry against the soft, green waves of the land. Paths carved into the hillside by thousands of feet over thousands of years stretched into the distance to either side. I love how paths draw us to them. They are a lifeline, offering safe passage across unknown terrain; a visible indication of the route many humans have taken before us. Our brains are wired to look for paths first, even before features such as boundaries and landmarks, to trust where others have trod.

On that day, on our quest to reach the highest point on the whole of this southern edge of the country, we followed the steepest paths ever onwards towards the top. At each junction we chose the clearest way up, starting on a gently sloping trail and later ascending on deep steps cut into the hillside. H, happy in his sling while I did the legwork, pointed out various things of interest along the way, which I attempted to name for him between laboured breaths. E, heroically, walked most of the way, with just a little assistance from Sim, whose strong arms swung her upwards every time she began to tire. Eventually we reached the summit, touching the trig point, breathing out into the view that stretched east to the hazy outline of Portland. It felt amazing to be high up, a gulls'-eye view of the world, the sparkling sea stretching ahead, the rolling green Dorset countryside behind, and the long line of the coast dividing the two.

There, on the highest point of the south coast, we chatted with the only other person there, a woman who had walked all the way from Portland and was continuing to walk westwards along the coast path. We shared our stories: hers of academia and lobbying major corporations to divest from fossil fuels; ours of our quest to experience the wilder side of our beautiful country while we still could, to try to live more lightly and to educate our children to do the same. It is amazing how often we have met and talked with people in places like this. Caught in a brief, shared moment somewhere out of the ordinary. Out of our ordinary.

*

As March drew on, the gaps between the rain grew longer and further apart. The earth began to dry at last, the mud less of an all-consuming problem. We returned from our walks without a heavy, sticky caking of mud covering our clothes and boots. And we no longer wore a wet, brown path into the grass as we walked to and from the tent. The days were also becoming noticeably longer, the mornings and evenings warmer and lighter and the nights less sharply cold. Our time in Uplyme was coming to an end and, as we talked about the warmer days ahead, our conversation came back to tents. Should we keep camping in the Emperor, now the weather was calmer? Or, would a smaller, lighter tent be better?

This wasn't the conversation about camping kit that we might have had in our pre-child days – about which was the lightest tent with the tiniest pack size that would make running for two days over rough terrain as easy as possible while still offering us somewhere dry to sleep. Now, our tent was quite literally the fabric of our existence. Our set-up determined so much about the safety, practicality and enjoyment of daily life. We had only budgeted for one pitch and the Casa alone was too small to live in for weeks at a time; really, we needed a smaller, more portable bell tent. One that would combine everything we loved about the Emperor – the tough yet breathable natural cotton canvas and airy, light space – but one that neither took up as much space when pitching or transporting it or had such a high risk of storm damage. But there was no way we could afford it.

One Monday morning – hiding in a café to plug everything in and get some quiet time to work while Sim took the kids to the beach – I reappeared from under the table with my various devices to find an email offering a solution we could never have dreamed of. A few days earlier I had emailed SoulPad, a Norfolk-based bell tent company, telling them about our trip and asking if they might be interested in working with us in some way. We had hoped they might be up for offering us a discount on a new bell tent in return for the publicity we would generate using it at the festivals we would be talking at later in the year.

The reply was from Zoe, one of the company's founders. They were offering us a four-metre bell tent, which they would arrange to be delivered to a convenient address for the start of April, for free. After all our severe financial troubles, it was an incredible piece of good news, and a gesture that would make such a huge difference to our year.

After the dark days of the bankruptcy, and the worry over the practicalities of our living arrangements as the year went on, this was just the stroke of good fortune we needed. I wrote an enthusiastic and very grateful reply and sat back with my coffee, feeling happier and more relaxed than I had done for weeks.

*

With a few days still to go until our new tent was due to arrive, and a window of fine, dry weather, we decided to pack away the Emperor and take our backpacking tent up onto Exmoor. We had been offered a couple of nights' camping for free not far from the village of Exford, high in the centre of the moor and near to the source of the River Exe, and it was somewhere we were both keen to know better.

It was mid-morning when we arrived, and the day was cold, clear and sunny. The young Exe snaked its way across open moorland, our campsite the soft grass of a semi-circle formed by one of the river's wide meanders. It felt remote and peaceful, with the ever-present music of the river in the background and bright spring flowers growing along the banks. To the north rose the highest, bleakest stretches of the moor, topped by Dunkery Beacon, the summit of the National Park at 519 metres. We pitched the little tent, unrolled camping mats and sleeping bags and set up our camping stove to boil water for coffee. With just the things we needed for a few nights' camping, it all felt so quick and easy compared to the usual lengthy process of setting up camp. We had a pump filter for water, which we collected from the river, then filtered and boiled. Wild garlic covered the ground in the tree-lined borders of our field – an abundant source of free leaves to add to our cooking. E liked to nibble them raw as she explored, weaving through the trees, making tiny bunches of daisies, and doing her best to creep up on the watchful bunnies that vanished underground the moment she got too near.

After a day exploring on foot, buying a few supplies from the nearby shop, we wrapped everyone up warmly and sat at the picnic bench outside the tent cooking pasta on our single burner stove. After supper it was too cold to sit outside for long, so we decided on an early night, E racing me to the washrooms to clean our teeth and then back to the tent to dive into our warm sleeping bags. Sim handed H over and I snuggled him in beside me, while Sim went to check the truck and the pegs. It felt like camping as we had once known it: light, easy, portable, adventurous. As we lay in the little tent in the fading light of a spring evening, the last of the day's birdsong echoed around the trees, the tawny owls began their evening hooting and the river rushed endlessly by. It was so perfect and so soothing, that, despite the early hour we all dozed off.

A few hours later I was wide awake, a startling, rasping roar of engines, squealing tyres, shouting and rough laughter dragging me from a deep sleep. Sim peered out through the tent door to see, illuminated in a pool of headlights, a group of lads in small, noisy cars gathering on the road that ran right past our tent. We lay still and sleepless in the darkness as the harsh, horrible sounds went on for hours, raking through the otherwise blissfully quiet night. I found myself gripping my face with my hands, desperate for rest, willing it to stop with all my being. By the time the peace of the moorland did eventually descend back on our campsite, the first light of the day had already begun to pale the canvas above us. The kids had slept well though, filled with their usual energy when they woke up, just moments after we had finally drifted off to sleep.

The following morning couldn't have been a more different experience of humanity, however. We had been invited to breakfast by an outdoor group that was staying at the hostel. It was mass catering, with queues of cheerful students lined up with plates and mugs, vats of baked beans, piles of sliced bread and urns of coffee – as different from our normal, peaceful morning routine as it was possible to imagine.

As we walked into the busy dining room, for a moment, I felt an overwhelming urge to run back to the tent, to retreat into my own, quiet space, sleep deprivation all but engulfing me. But we sat down and soon found ourselves surrounded by a big, noisy group, chatting and laughing about the experiences they had shared over the past week. I soon realised that, far from being overwhelming, it was just what we needed to revive us after our disturbed night.

The room was warm and the group welcoming. We ended up staying for over an hour, sharing breakfast and conversation, E chatting away happily, telling everyone about living in a tent, H attracting lots of attention with his big smiles. So often I felt distanced from others, when our situation was so different from theirs, as if I needed to protect us from criticism or judgement. But here, surrounded by friendliness and acceptance, I realised more than ever how much I needed, and valued, the human connections we were making along the way.

We stayed one more night on Exmoor, this time enjoying the tranquil sounds of nature as we dozed off and sleeping soundly until the sun woke us, bright and warm on the canvas the following morning. After breakfast we set out to explore the surrounding moorland, climbing to the top of Dunkery Beacon and challenging ourselves to find Joaney How and Robin How, the hill's two Bronze Age burial mounds. All around the empty moor rolled away into distance, meeting at its edges a sky of cloudless blue. Skylarks rose from the heather, filling the air with their burbling song, while far below stood the ancient oaks of Horner Wood, still leafless and softly brown. Later, tired but happy to have soaked up so much of the essence of this place, we ambled back to the campsite and packed away. Then we drove south to Dartmoor for the final time until we returned in the autumn, excited by the news that our brand-new tent was already there waiting for us.

Unfurling
Springtime on Dartmoor

FOR ALL THE TIME we had spent getting to know it, the weather still had the power to surprise us. It was late March on Dartmoor and we awoke to snow. We stepped out of the tent into a dreamlike world of glittering snowflakes, swirling about us, covering the grass and tracks, settling softly on the tent's canvas with the quietest of whispers. The distant, high stretches of the moor were already blanketed white, standing out starkly against an iron-grey sky, line drawn trees inked in stark black contrast.

Sim and I were as excited as the children. Before we had even had breakfast we were out, searching for the places where the snow was deepest. Wrapped in warm layers, we ran through a muffled landscape, our voices strange, dead sound with no echo. We climbed upwards, finding the snow, finding the views, breathing in the cold, clear, clean air.

But the sharp, icy wind was also awaiting us at the top of the ridge, springing from its cover as we crested the long wave of the land, meeting us full force, face on. We were unprepared for the sudden, startling cold, our bodies and minds already settling into spring.

'Quick – let's get back to the tent!' I shouted, the wind whipping my words away as I hugged E to me to shelter her from the icy onslaught. We turned and ran back down the hill, H bouncing in Sim's arms, laughing as we went, shaking the snow from our clothes and boots as we reached the tent. Within minutes all four of us were huddled back in bed, rosy cheeks, smiles and laughter all round as we warmed up. In the end it was the briefest of wintery visits: by the following morning all trace of snow had vanished, spring returning to our world.

Keen to try out our beautiful new SoulPad bell tent, we had spent the past week on the eastern edge of the moor, enjoying a peaceful pitch on a basic campsite. Other than Easter weekend, when we had been joined by a small group of couples in tents who had kept to themselves, we were once again the only campers.

A few minutes' walk away, at the opposite side of the field, were a composting toilet and outdoor shower. The shower was a revelation: the combination of a cold, easterly wind and cascades of hot water on bare skin utterly glorious. Until, that is, one morning when the hot water system broke, and I was left standing naked in the biting air with only a fine spray of freezing cold water firing out of the showerhead.

The new tent was perfect though. We were keen to use this time to test it out properly, before venturing further afield, getting to know how best to pitch it, how it stood up to the scouring moorland winds and how to arrange everything in it as we were downsizing considerably. And it was exactly as we had hoped: smaller and more aerodynamic than the Emperor, yet with the same qualities of natural light and airiness. The living space was round rather than rectangular, which made it easier to use somehow and gave us plenty of room even when filled with our table and boxes and duffle bags. It also helped that we wouldn't be using the woodburner inside any longer, choosing instead to cook outside on our double burner camping stove. This had worked well during our time in the South Hams earlier in the year, and we certainly wouldn't miss the constant stress of managing the fire and small children within the confines of a tent, or the smokiness and lengthy process of lighting the stove which took up so much of each day.

Despite the coldness of the nights, and having no heating at all, it surprised me how well we all slept. Lying on our thick mattresses beneath layers of duvet and blanket, we were insulated from every angle, the heat of our four bodies trapped safely inside. H was feeding less during the nights now, and this, combined with the freedom from constantly worrying about our debts meant sleeping in the tent was almost always a good experience.

We had pegged out the tarp we had used with the Emperor over the entrance to the new tent and stashed our boots and boxes beneath it. It all felt immensely peaceful, surrounded by birdsong and the fresh, spring scents of grass and moss and newly budding woodland. After a week of work deadlines, when I had felt an almost constant pressure to fill every available gap with productivity, we were now able to relax a little and enjoy settling back into our familiar, comfortable rhythm.

*

As we lived our lives in and around the tent – cooking over the little stove, playing, working, sleeping – the moor was always there. I was constantly aware of its presence, intriguing, beguiling, calling from just beyond the hedged boundaries of the field.

One morning, hearing the sounds of the moor awakening through the canvas, I left the tent early, taking a restless H with me, warm in his sling and a padded suit with cosy boots. The long grass, as I strode across it, was crunchy with a frost coating. Our breath rose in plumes, mingling in the still air. We reached the edge of the field and carried on through a gap in the hedge into a wilder corner, bordered by trees growing so close together that, with our combined width, we could barely squeeze between their trunks.

The sounds of Dartmoor were everywhere: the trickle of water through granite bedrock; the lively twitter of birds; distant sheep and cows; the whoosh and whisper of the wind flying over high moorland, tuned and tangled in the knotty branches of ancient woods. We startled a green woodpecker, which rose from the grass ahead making its coarse, yaffling cry. H reached out a small, inquisitive hand for some thick, bright moss, illuminated by the morning sun, that clung to the branches, delighting in its soft damp fuzziness on his skin. Snug in his cocoon, half fabric and half my skin, he had the choice of reaching out into the world, making new discoveries of light, colour and texture, or retreating inwards to warmth and familiarity.

I loved to watch our children exploring and getting to know the world around them by engaging with it physically and emotionally, with all their senses. It was hard to stop myself from intervening sometimes, when they picked up an insect with clumsy fingers to examine it more closely or pulled the petals from a flower. I knew they did not mean to be cruel or destructive, but were simply figuring out how things worked – the mechanics of life. Sometimes I had to step in, with the inevitable furious consequences, but I tried as much as possible to leave them to experiment and discover their world in their own way.

E often played on her own for half an hour or more in a far corner of the field, gently testing the distance between us. I noticed she was becoming fractionally more independent as each day passed, like a flower that starts as a tiny bud, wrapped up within itself, but in time opens its arms to embrace and engage with the world.

Watching my children that day, I thought about how different the bond we shared was to the one I had with Sim. The bond between me and my children thrives on being tested and stretched – it is their job to pull and challenge, and mine to always stay steadfast. They must know that whatever they do, wherever they go, whoever they are and for as long as I can be, I will always be here for them. My bond with Sim isn't like that. We both have an equal responsibility to maintain and to nurture it, never testing it too much, never stretching it beyond its natural level of comfort. We are acutely aware of both its strength and its fragility.

People often ask how we cope with living, working and parenting together, rarely spending more than a couple of hours apart on any day. The answer: it just works and yet we work hard at it. Although we are, in many ways, different people, we share the same passions. And we champion, celebrate and encourage each other. I am as happy – happier perhaps – when Sim achieves something that matters to him than when I do so myself. Far from driving us apart, the more time we spend together, the better we seem able to make it all work.

*

We had made it a part of our daily routine – me in the mornings, Sim in the afternoons – to run to the top of the ridge to make contact with the outside world. As no signal reached us in the valley, unable to penetrate the granite bedrock of the hills, checking email meant putting on my trainers and running up the winding track from the campsite to the top. I loved that run, legs and lungs screaming by the time the pips of signal filtered through to my phone. But when the weather prevented us making this twice-daily trip, it could be frustrating to find an email with a last-minute request from an editor that we'd been too late to accept, thus losing us vital work.

Slowly but surely though, we were finding more requests for work coming in. In the early months, when we were establishing ourselves as writers, with a new book to promote and a publishers' contract to honour, we did a lot of work for free in return for the exposure. But now, we were more often than not offered payment for work, or at least were brave enough to ask for it. Finally, our income was getting more regular and stable.

We had also begun discussions with a publisher about our second book, which was to be about family adventures around the UK, a subject in which we felt we were rapidly acquiring expertise. It helped to keep our trip feeling like an adventure, too, as we looked at the weeks and months ahead in the context of this new project. We made sure to capture scenes, moments and details in our photography, knowing that these pictures might soon be part of a book.

I was growing to love the whole process of producing a piece of work, from the first glimmers of an idea, through the writing, editing, shaping and reshaping, through to a finished article. It didn't always go well, though. I am a fierce self-critic, always feeling I can do better, often surprised by positive responses to my work. But even I was taken aback by a reply from an editor at a major newspaper, who had approached us for an article, offering us a good rate of pay. I had written very little for the national press at the time and instantly felt choked by the pressure. How could I possibly produce anything close to the polished, witty, fact-packed travel articles other people wrote? I couldn't sleep or think about anything else for days, but neither could I write, frozen into inactivity by an overwhelming, all-encompassing sense of impending failure and humiliation.

On deadline day, I sat miserable and alone in the café of an art gallery in our corner of Dartmoor, which we had come to know well. We retreated there in bad weather for good coffee, free WiFi, books and toys and it was a place where I had had many a telephone meeting. While Sim entertained the kids at a nearby park, I forced the words for the article out, read them with increasing dread and horror, then emailed them off to the editor. Surely it was better to send something, than nothing at all?

Sim was his usual positive and reassuring self, even though I hadn't let him read a word. 'It'll be great . . . It always is. I bet she'll love it.'

It wasn't great.

And she didn't love it.

Back came an email with my pathetic attempt at writing attached, interspersed everywhere with giant red capital letters. At one point I had referred to a 'grassy meadow', to which the editor had added, in bright red type, 'ALL MEADOWS ARE GRASSY!!!' The worst thing was that as I went through her comments, I agreed with every one: my writing was terrible.

Crippled by self-doubt, I had messed up, throwing away what many aspiring travel writers would have considered the opportunity of a lifetime. The truth was I wasn't ready. The idea of thousands of people reading my words, potentially comparing them with the words of writers I so admired, made me both deeply uncomfortable and terrified. Often, impostor syndrome is unjustified but, on this occasion, I was an imposter. In the end, I took many valuable lessons from that experience, including how not to respond when someone sends me a piece of their writing. And I will never again refer to a *grassy meadow* as long as I live.

*

As the days continued to grow lighter and warmer, Dartmoor unfurled itself into a place buzzing, twittering and scuffling with life. The lower slopes of the moor were bright with bluebells and primroses. Trees that only days ago had stood bare and still as winter now fluttered with brand new leaves. At around five-thirty in the morning, as the canvas above us turned from darkness to the blue of dawn, then to the gold of sunrise, the birds began to sing. There were the rough tones of crows, rooks, jackdaws and ravens, the hollow monotony of wood pigeons and, gradually building, a wave of twittering, lilting birdsong from which it was hard to pick out any individual call.

Walking from the tent we spotted deer, rabbits and hundreds of birds. We made a list with E, adding to it each time we spotted a new bird on the moor or on our trips into the valley or out to the coast. It was already long: yellowhammers, stone chats, cirl buntings, wagtails, flycatchers, treecreepers, rock pipits, blue tits, great tits and coal tits, nuthatches, robins, woodpeckers, wrens, pigeons, blackbirds, thrushes . . . Buzzards scribed wide circles over our heads, wide wings glinting gold against the sky. We often heard cuckoos and occasionally saw them, scything through the air – a sharp streak of striped gunmetal-grey. We found nests hidden deep within hedgerows and holes in walls, stuck under eaves and piled in messy heaps high up in the branches of bigger trees. E was becoming quite an expert at pointing them out herself, and it filled me with joy to hear her identifying each one, growing in confidence with each success. Our list grew longer. How many would we add by the end of our wild year?

With sunnier weather and H more settled in my absence, I ran further than I had for more than a year, covering the ground under my own steam, feeling the miles gradually drawing the strength from my body, replacing it with an earned tiredness that I enjoyed. I have often felt that being a runner gives me a clear identity, aside from being a mother or even being a woman. When I am out running, dressed in running kit, that's all people see: a runner. I like the simplicity of that. It is also an easier guise for me, my body lending itself to running in a way it never has to dresses, heels and the critical eye of the mirror. In some ways I find being a mother affords a similar sense of anonymity. People see me with my children and the picture is complete: I am a mother. Nothing more, nothing less. Move on.

*

Looking back on the first six months of our wild year I felt a mixture of emotions. We had, without any doubt, experienced many of the best moments of our lives, but there had also been some dark times – times of physical, emotional and financial hardship that had challenged us to our limits. Although I perhaps would not have chosen to go through these challenges, I was incredibly proud of the way we had faced and overcome them together, and I knew we were stronger for it.

Now it was almost time to leave to head north, packing up our lives and taking everything we would need for four to five months of camping, apart from what we could restock along the way. But first, we wanted one last wild camp, out on the moor, far from any person or building.

On a warm April evening, we packed a big rucksack, filling it with our backpacking tent, sleeping bags, stove, food and water.

Usually, when we wild camped, we did so in the shelter of the valley, near to the cottage. But this time we walked high up onto the moor, following clear paths that gradually became sheep tracks before disappearing altogether and leaving us wading through a sea of bracken. H watched a pair of buzzards circling in the evening sky, his eyes following the birds round and round, their thin, mewing cries mingling with our conversation and E's excited chatter. She rode high on Sim's shoulders, one hand shading her eyes from the evening sun, which made a halo of her blonde curls against a silk-screen backdrop of the fading, distant hills.

After nearly two hours of walking, we found our spot, invisible from roads or houses, sheltered by a tall pile of rough, granite boulders and not far from a small stream. By this time the sky had filled with dark clouds, heavy with rain. I held a sleeping H while Sim quickly pitched the tent, E handing out pegs to secure our tiny scrap of fabric to the moorland floor. Then we unrolled our mats and shook out our sleeping bags, making everything ready for the night.

At first it was a barely noticeable condensing of the mist, gathering in tiny droplets on our hair and clothes. But, as we clambered into our precious dry shelter, our bodies quickly raising the temperature inside, the rain began to fall in earnest, splashing off the foliage, drumming the boulders, and pattering on the canvas. We sat just inside the door of the tent, staying dry with our feet in the porch, sharing hot chocolate from a flask and gazing out across the valley through the moving veil of rain to the rocky outcrops of the tors, dark against a pale sky. Eventually, chilled by the wind and rain, we zipped ourselves in for the night. It was some of the wildest weather we had camped out in for a while. Though sheltered by the rocks, we were still high up on open land, several degrees colder than the valley, exposed to the winds that fled unhindered across the moor.

I found it hard to sleep at first, lying still in the darkness, alert and listening. When I did, every time the wind whipped the tent fabric I woke up with a start, ready for fight or flight. Rationally, I knew we were safe – safer, probably, than on any campsite – and yet I was unable to tune out the unfamiliar sounds and the weight of responsibility for having chosen this very spot out of all the other possibilities. What if it was, somehow, the wrong one? Finally, we all managed to sleep, waking to a morning fresh and bright and sparkling in the sunlight after the overnight rain. We shared flapjacks, made coffee in the Jetboil and enjoyed the view. It had only been one night but, on the long walk off the moor that morning, I felt deeply rewilded.

On our return, the packing for the next few months began in earnest. It felt like a turning point in our year, which had, after the stormy, first few months, started to feel almost comfortable. From now on, though, it wouldn't be so easy to rely on the safety of Dartmoor should anything go wrong. Or call in at the cottage for supper or duct tape. In the coming months, we would be far more on our own, far more reliant on ourselves and each other.

Our plan was to make our way north slowly, minimising each day's driving and enjoying the places along the way rather than speeding past them, focused on a single destination. We'd visit my dad in Bristol and my mum and my sister in the Midlands, then spend a few nights in the Peak District. From there we'd continue to the Lakes, where we planned to spend a month or more before winding our way back southwards to our summer pitch in the Welsh borders. If everything went to plan, we wouldn't be returning to Dartmoor until September.

With a mixture of excitement and trepidation we packed the truck, trying to be ruthless about what we took – or rather what we didn't take – so it all fitted in and was to hand if we needed it on the way. It helped that our new bell tent was so much smaller, but space was still going to be tight. We reduced our clothing even further, and limited ourselves to a pair of boots, a pair of off-road running shoes and a pair of flipflops each. I had long ago learnt that flipflops make campsite shower floors more bearable. We fitted in as many books and toys for the kids as we could – it would be a long time before we would be able to replenish them again.

By the time darkness was falling on the moor around us, the truck was all packed up, the back door closing with only a little extra persuasion. In the morning, we would squeeze our backpacking tent, sleeping bags and mats into the last remaining space – beneath the children's feet – and then we'd be ready. Ready for the next stage of our adventure.

Northbound

Friendships and first steps in the Peak District

Hᴵᴳᴴ ᴏɴ ᴍʏ ʟɪꜱᴛ of least favourite things is being stuck in a car, on a busy motorway, with two unhappy children. Long car journeys have always been difficult, and we still avoid them as much as we can. Whenever we had to travel any distance by car, E and H fiercely resisted being strapped into their seats and we had to stop so often that journeys took twice as long as they should. I could never understand why other people's children loved cars and went straight to sleep. Often, we had to stop every half an hour as H would only sit still for that long before starting to scream.

That may well have been partly to do with me. I spent these journeys in a state of intense anxiety, convinced imminent disaster awaited us around every bend. In my early twenties, I had been in a car in a head-on collision with a lorry. While I have no memory of the collision itself – I wasn't driving and was looking away at the moment of impact – the seconds afterwards, when the lorry was pushing our car towards the edge of a cliff, are as vivid in my imagination as if they happened yesterday. I watched the drop coming fast towards me out of my window, utterly powerless to do anything about it. I remember an overwhelming sadness, more powerful than I had ever felt anything before, knowing I wasn't ready to die. In the end, which turned out not to be the end, we stopped just in time, inches short of the edge of the cliff. I escaped with a few broken bones and a vivid film of those seconds, which I had believed would be my last, burned into my memory. That film has never dimmed in its clarity or ferocity, and writing about it brings back a surge of adrenaline and nausea. I had passed my driving test only weeks before, and every time I attempted to drive afterwards it haunted me – I would arrive at my destination so exhausted all I wanted to do was sleep.

Perhaps I could have sought help for the fear that roads and cars bring, to try to make every journey less of an ordeal. To me, though, it doesn't feel like an irrational fear, but one backed up by facts that means I'll never consider cars as the easy option, and never drive somewhere when I could go on foot, bike, or train. Living in a world crowded with cars, and breathing air polluted by them, I choose to accept my mental scarring and use it to impassion my conviction that cars should be a backup plan, not a default one.

Having been through that experience also makes me even more aware of the privilege of being alive, of having choices and of loving and being loved. It changed my life in an instant. I stopped wasting time in dead-end jobs and started my degree.

I stopped drinking and started running every day and through that found a new respect for my body. In the weeks after the crash I could barely walk for five minutes before the pain became so intense I had to lie down. But, from that low starting point, I gradually built up to a point where I could happily run for three or four hours at a time. I expect, in many ways, the life we were now living with the children was part of the legacy of that crash.

My car-related fears were also part of the reason, along with the prohibitive costs, why we had never considered a campervan for our adventures. I needed to escape the car after a long journey and retreat to the airy peace of a tent, sleeping against the solid earth with the movement of the air and the sounds of the outdoors all around. My favourite pitches, while they were always harder work at the start and finish, were those where we had to leave the truck behind and camp far away from the sight, sound and stench of engines.

Setting out on our slow journey north, we stopped off at Taunton Leisure in Exeter, the outdoor shop where Sim and I met when we worked there together years before. It was fun to visit, catching up with familiar faces and remembering old times. There's something about a good outdoor shop – the static swish of Nylon and the earthy scent of leather; the striped, tightly coiled ropes and racks of climbing hardwear jangling with possibility. We both found ourselves gazing longingly at all the shiny things far beyond our budget. But for the kids' bored irritation, we could have browsed those treasure-clad walls all morning.

In the end we bought some spare gas canisters and two camping chairs, for which, after so many months of kneeling and crouching in the tent, my grumbling knees had been longing. Sim bought a replacement pair of walking boots, his second of the year so far. I was pleased with my own boots, a pair of lightweight yet sturdy Salomons, which seemed to be holding out impressively well by comparison.

We spent three evenings in warm, welcoming company: the first with my dad and stepmum, the second at my mum's house, and the third with my sister and her partner. So far it had all gone perfectly to plan, staying a night with each of my family members having got us as far as Birmingham with only fairly short drives in-between. We left my sister's after lunch, optimistic about the possibility of making it to our campsite in the Peak District in one go.

An hour later, we were sitting in stationary traffic on the motorway, having only made it a couple of miles down the road. Already, E and H were bored and miserable in the back. They were hungry but didn't want any of the food we had with us. They were tired but refused to go to sleep. They were used to being outside, grass beneath their feet and the wind in their hair and found the stuffy confines of their car seats unbearable.

Eventually, after multiple stops and several hours of driving slower than walking pace, we pulled into a service station somewhere in Leicestershire. It was getting late. To the west, the sun was setting over a skyline of industrial buildings. I was so tired, so wrung out after hours of placating the kids and poorly managing my own anxieties. We had a deadline for a magazine article the following morning, and I had been planning to spend the evening writing, but already there was no evening left. I was sitting in the front seat feeding H, while Sim searched for alternative route that avoided the motorway, when I spotted a hotel next to the service station. It was one of those soulless, generic hotels but, at that moment, all I could think about was not having to wrestle H back into his seat yet again.

'Why don't we just see if there's a room here?' I said tentatively to Sim. 'We need to work. We need sleep . . . I don't think I can face any more roads today.'

'Here . . . ?' Sim's voice was filled with doubt. I could sense his loathing for the place, for the waste of money, for the idea of giving up when we were really so close to a campsite that was in character a million miles from here.

He leant forward, rubbing his face with the palms of his hands. When he sat up again, there were tears in his eyes, something I had rarely seen. In my desperation to be away from the roads I had jumped at the chance to simply stop, but Sim was devastated. He, too, was so weary from never quite getting enough sleep, from having spent the day driving surrounded by so much stress both inside and outside the car. And he felt a sense of failure, far more strongly than I did, on these occasions when we weren't able to camp. While he knew there were times when it was the most sensible thing to do, and times when having the kids with us meant we had to make decisions that were best for them, even when they were at odds with our plans, it hit him hard. And this was a long way from our dream of spending every night for a whole year under canvas. I pulled my beloved man over to me with my spare arm and we held each other for a while, wishing it would all feel better.

Half an hour later, the kids were in the bath, the kettle was on, and various parts of the tent hung drying about the hotel room. I sat at the desk working furiously on our article with all our electrical equipment plugged in around me. Later, we had a picnic, sitting together on the big double bed, with fresh white baguettes and other extravagantly exciting things from the M&S Food next door – if we were going to do this, we were going to make the most of it. We let the kids watch cartoons on the TV that took up most of one wall before they eventually dozed off, then tucked them in, tiny and peaceful in the giant expanse of the bed.

In the end we finished working at 2 a.m., finally switching off the laptop and collapsing into fitful sleep, the room too hot, too stuffy. Still, we were convinced we had done the right thing: the hotel might have cost several times what we usually spent on a night's accommodation, but there was no doubt we had got our money's worth and the kids had loved it.

The following morning, we finally made it to the Peak District. We had booked back into North Lees, the same campsite where, ten months earlier, we had come up with the idea of moving into a tent. Our corner of the field was a lush patch of grass surrounded by newly unfurling ferns and bracken. Edging the site, freshly leafed beech, birch and larch trees rose from a woodland floor scattered with bluebells. Winding through these, a path led up to a flight of steps and a gate, which opened onto the craggy edges and moors above. The rush of the stream, the hollow calls of cuckoos and the bleating of brand-new lambs filled the valley – it was a perfect picture of spring.

The site was set out on two levels, with a few small tents pitched in the lower field, mainly climbers enjoying its proximity to the gritstone at Stanage, but the upper field was empty when we arrived. With the agreement of the site staff, we pitched both the bell tent and our backpacking tent, affording us the luxury of a light, airy space for the daytime and a cosy retreat at night.

Unzipping the tent door early each morning onto a landscape that sparkled in the sunshine, it was impossible not to feel infused with excitement about the day ahead. The nights were cold again and fat droplets of dew covered our tents, showering off in a fine rainbow spray when we shook the fabric. I couldn't believe how much of a difference the new chairs made to my daily life, giving my poor knees a much-needed break from being constantly bent while I crouched, crawled, knelt or sat on the floor. I could now stretch my legs out in front of me with my knees straight – a luxury I had never thought to appreciate before. A stack of two boxes now made a table of about the right height to work at while sitting in a chair or I could comfortably sit with my laptop on my lap. Having always been grumpy about how much of our lives we are expected to spend in chairs, their absence had reminded me that, in moderation, they can be a very good thing.

The morning hours passed easily as we took it in turns to work or wandered across the lane to see the lambs in the field with E and H. Further entertainment came from a group of cheerful volunteers who arrived each day to repair the drystone walls. In the afternoons, we explored further afield, walking up the steep steps to emerge below Stanage, watching as climbers made their way up the rock faces. We reminisced about the trips we'd made here when it had just been the two of us, wondering how long it would be before we could put E and H into child-sized full body harnesses and take them on some climbing adventures of their own.

Our stay in the Peak District also coincided with H's first birthday. We all made him cards and bought a present each from E and us. He opened these with eager fingers and delighted sounds, which, each day, were becoming more like words. After breakfast in the tent, we walked across the fields to the village of Hathersage in search of birthday cake, something I had decided not to attempt on the camping stove. We had arranged to meet up with my friend, Sarah, who lived nearby and who we had barely seen since our wedding. It made the day even more special to sit close in the warmth of a café and share stories from the past months. It reminded me how precious those friendships are which instantly, even after months or even years apart, feel as close as they always have done.

H turning one felt like a milestone for both him and me. He had been a baby when we moved into the tent, but now he was standing up on his own, crawling at speed, feeding himself and making his opinions and wishes clearly known. It was strange to think that he had spent half his life living in this wild and nomadic way, although he was, of course, completely oblivious to there being any other way. He had even taken his first few unsupported steps that morning, as if to mark the occasion, just as his sister had done on her first birthday nearly three years before.

That evening, back at the tent, lying in the darkness surrounded by the soft sounds of our little world within and the wider world outside, I thought back to those days a year ago. I remembered the hugeness of my body just before H was born, the intensity of the afternoon of his birth and the surprising differences in the experience of welcoming a second child into our lives when, unlike the first time around, it was not all so completely and terrifyingly new. I remembered the delight and relaxed enjoyment I was able to feel for this new baby in those first two weeks before Sim had to go back to work, savouring every moment of his freshly baked newness. He would sleep in the crook of my knee while I worked, recline in a beanbag while I played with E or lie along the length of Sim's forearm, his tiny head cradled in Sim's hand.

Apart from the nausea of the first few weeks and the lumbering discomfort of the final month, pregnancy had been a novel and enjoyable time for me. I was lucky to have had relatively straightforward pregnancies. Both times, being pregnant had freed me from my long-held narratives around my body and the strict routines of training and fuelling that had been a part of my life for so long. I embraced my growing weight and the ever-increasing space my body inhabited in a way I could never have done in any other context.

I realised, six months into our wild year, that again my body had vanished from my own noticing. I had barely looked in a mirror since we had left, never felt guilty about having too much food or too little exercise. Our life had moved away from a place where these concerns were even possible. Food was precious, and we only had what we could fit in alongside everything else we needed, so although we never went hungry, there was often only just enough. Simply existing was harder work too, at every moment of every day, from just staying warm to the length of the walk required for everything from going to the toilet to collecting a container full of water, to cooking. But, for all its toughness, we relished this way of life.

It felt good to be back in the Peak District, exploring its familiar landscapes, visiting places we knew well from the past and discovering others that were new. One evening we walked up the steps from the campsite and along Stanage Edge. It was warm for May, a dusky haze softening both the gritstone landscape and our moods. To one side, level with our path, stretched the bleak expanse of Hallam and Burbage Moors; to the other the land dropped away, sharply at first down the vertical rock of the edge and then rolling away into the soft, hazy distance.

As we walked, pointing out familiar landmarks as we went, a movement to one side caught my attention. There above the moorland, impossibly pale against the darkening backdrop, were two barn owls, hunting. They were at once powerful and yet ethereal, one moment like petals floating on the evening breeze, the next fast and deadly, dropping to the moor below, like a stone caught in a silk scarf. It was one of those magical evenings – the hazy warmth, the softly heather-scented air, the landscape unfolding all around us and the two majestic birds, weaving their dance together across the moor.

As if drawing a line beneath that evening, for the next few days, the rain fell solidly, a mesmerising, ceaseless patter on the tent all around, all day, all night. We were glad to have both tents up, giving us a change of scenery and more indoor space to wait out the rain. There was no electric hook-up and no WiFi and we were relieved to have H's new toys and the fresh selection of books and DVDs we had brought with us from Devon. We ventured out for an hour or so every day, fully waterproofed against the storms, but it was difficult to dry everything out afterwards. On the third wet day, yearning for something else to do, we headed for Bakewell, where we knew there was a good library. We spent most of the day there, reading to the kids, catching up on work and emails.

One email was particularly frustrating. We had written a piece for a newspaper, which had been published weeks earlier, and had been given a date to expect payment which had come and gone. I had chased the payment up the previous day, and now had an email from a woman who worked in the finance department explaining that there had been a delay and, having missed the deadline for this month's payroll, it would be another month before the money would be in our account. It was only £300, but for us that was an entire month's budget for accommodation or food and its absence meant everything to us right then. I clicked the reply button, knowing being angry and upset wouldn't help but at the same time wondering how this woman would feel she had just discovered she wouldn't be getting paid this month. But how honest should I be? Should I say this meant we would struggle to pay both our accommodation and food costs this month? I typed out my reply, explaining that we were self-employed and on a very low income and that we were therefore absolutely dependent on being paid on time. Was there any way she could put it through sooner? I hit send, hoping for the best but knowing from past experiences that it was unlikely the mistake would be rectified any time soon.

By the time we left the library and set off back to the campsite I'd had no reply. Perhaps she felt she had done all she could and had nothing more to add. It was a depressing end to an otherwise enjoyable and productive day, a much-needed break from the rainy confines of the tent. I hated how much power those managing our payments had over us. That if the person whose job it was to process payments happened to be away, or there was a computer problem, or someone somewhere hadn't filled in the right form – the list of reasons we were given was lengthy – we would not get paid when we were supposed to. It happened over and over again, making our already stretched budget even harder to manage. In my darkest moments I wanted to go and knock on these people's doors, asking them what we were supposed to do, what they would do in our situation. At brighter times I remembered the Robert Benchley quote: 'The freelance writer is a man who is paid per piece or per word or perhaps.'

We had hoped to find a laundrette in Bakewell, filling the back of the truck with bags of washing as we left the tent. But the only offering was service washes, meaning they would do the work for us for a little over £25. At that moment, so much down on our expected budget, we just couldn't afford it, so we took it all back to the campsite again. We had to find a laundrette soon, but until then we'd just have to make do.

Finally, on our last full day at the campsite, the rain stopped and we awoke to sun shining through the canvas, warm on our faces like a, soothing, healing embrace. Outside, the world looked clean and vivid, freshly washed after all the rain. It felt glorious to be warm and dry and we made the most of it, spending the day packing for the following morning and enjoying not having to go anywhere. Later, we cooked outside and sat long into the evening watching bats bug-hunting in the dusky air.

We had arranged to spend the second week of our Peak District stay on a campsite in Hayfield, on the western edge of the national park. The campsite was more commercial than the peaceful meadow we had just left, with a few campers in tents and vans already pitched. But it was friendly and clean, and perfectly positioned for exploring the moors around Kinder reservoir and the western slopes of the Kinder plateau. The weather was more settled now and there was plenty in and around the campsite to keep the children happy, including a playground, a flock of friendly ducks, and chickens and rabbits that were so tame the children were able to get within a few steps of them.

With such easy entertainment, Sim and I were able to take it in turns to run further, sometimes for two or three hours at a time, following sweeping trails over sheep-cropped fellsides, climbing steep stony tracks to find the best views, delighting in the freedom and hard physical exertion of it all. This was where I had first learnt to run over rough ground and in high, wild places. I loved the rise and fall and flow of the landscape and how it made me feel to run fast across it. Now I was fit from our daily life and regular training, running felt like flying. For the first time since H arrived, I felt like myself again.

Each day we ground our coffee in a small hand grinder. Beans kept better and were easier to transport than ground coffee, and much less likely to find their way out of their container and into everything else in one of our big food boxes. It had become a pleasant ritual, which we fondly referred to as the Daily Grind, sitting in the doorway of the tent turning the handle as the beans gradually disappeared from the top half of the machine and ended up a soft, brown powder in the glass container at the bottom.

A few days into our stay in Hayfield, I was part-way through this process when a family arrived on bikes, with two boys around E's age on the back of their parents' bikes. Though it was getting warmer by the day, it was still rare to meet other families camping, particularly with younger children. Those we had come across, weekending in campervans or in groups with other families, also in campervans, had made us feel different – weird even – in our draughty canvas home. But there was something about this family – recognition, perhaps, of a similar approach to life – and we clicked straight away.

Sandy and Andy were friendly and smiley and seemed genuinely interested in our trip. They shared their own stories of long-distance cycling adventures with their children. E, fearless and sociable as ever, got on well with their boys and they spent the day playing games and roaming around the site. It was good to see her enjoying the company of other children, and for us to have like-minded company, too.

The week flew by and soon the time came, once again, for us to head north. It was a gloriously warm and sunny morning and we lingered over our porridge, then over coffee, enjoying talking over old adventures with our new friends. Eventually, they left for the day on their bikes and we packed the tent away. We had wanted to avoid leaving early so as not to get caught up in the busy commuter traffic, but in the end, it was well past eleven by the time we were ready to leave.

I walked around the flattened grass where our tent had been pitched, scanning the ground carefully to make sure we hadn't left anything behind. A lost peg could be frustrating, a lost toy disastrous, so we had learnt it was always worth checking.

Finding nothing, I wandered back to the truck, feeling the now familiar thrill of exhilaration at this being our whole existence, right now. Everything we needed to live comfortably was packed into this small space – this was our reality, our home. And, despite the difficulties of ensuring we were paid on time, our dream of working for ourselves was slowly becoming a reality. Was the plan that had seemed so crazy a year ago actually beginning to work?

SUMMER

'Why, what is to live? Not to eat and drink and breathe,— but to feel the life in you down all the fibres of being, passionately and joyfully.'

Elizabeth Barrett Browning.

Weathering
Highs and lows in the Lake District

THE FIRST TIME I visited the Lakes, aged seventeen, I was utterly captivated by the mountains. I still remember the exact feeling, sitting in the back of a friend's aging Volvo as we rattled up the motorway, gazing out at the rolling green fells, which seemed to grow more and more massive as we drove between them. I was awestruck, mesmerised, aching to be out there, up there; to know what that *felt* like.

I've heard many people describe their first experiences of mountains in a similar way – like love at first sight, or perhaps even obsession. But why should we feel like this about a feature of the landscape that is so far removed from safety and comfort? Places that can be hostile and dangerous to our warm, soft bodies and easily disorientated minds? I understand our love of paths and trails and why we feel compelled to follow them, but our fascination with mountains is harder to explain.

And yet I feel the same way each and every time I return to the Lakes, or any mountainous area, to run or climb, or amble at the pace of a small child. In *The Living Mountain*, Nan Shepherd describes perfectly that astonishment brought about by mountains; how, no matter how often we explore them, we never grow accustomed to them.

The excitement of being back in the Lakes grew steadily as we wound our way along the road through Great Langdale, watching the fells grow darker, higher and more rugged to either side. Our campsite lay at the far end of the valley, nestled below the jagged pillars of the Langdale Pikes, and we heard their whispers calling us to their high places the moment we stepped out of the truck.

We pitched the bell tent in a corner of the main field, hoping the dense hedge behind would shelter us from both the heat of the sun and the full force of any wind or rain. That evening, just before the sun faded behind the tops drawing a cool veil of soft grey across the valley, the shadows of the surrounding trees painted a new picture of this new place on the canvas.

The next morning, busy around the tent making coffee and breakfast, I watched the orange light of the sun flow over the folds and crevices of the mountains surrounding us with a thrill of excitement. To our west, where Scafell Pike lay hidden behind Bowfell and Crinkle Crags, the tops were still covered in cloud, as if, still beneath a fluffy duvet, they were yet to get out of bed.

Sim and I were both desperate to run this alluring skyline. This is the kind of terrain Sim loves to run over. He is nimble as a goat and his strong legs making light work of the ascents and descents. He is happy out in the mountains alone, whatever the weather, while I must admit to being more of a fair-weather mountain runner. I love the far-reaching views, the contrasting landscape suffused with colour and etched with dark shadows in the rocky nooks and cracks that a sunny day in the Lakes brings. Sim runs for the physical and logistical challenges it brings; I love the physicality too, but I also run to think and feel in the multi-dimensional, multi-sensory way only possible through movement in wild places.

We took it in turns to run from the tent, exploring the Cumbria Way, scaling the airy, rocky summits of the Langdale Pikes and exploring the remote depths of Mickleden. One day I ran to Grasmere, over the top and steeply down into the village, then back up again to Easdale Tarn for a swim, returning to the tent hours later, hot and tired but deeply happy.

But I also realised I needed to be careful with these longer, harder runs. I needed to have energy left to be fully there for the kids and would berate myself if I ran too hard or too far, leaving myself over-tired and lacking in patience. In this uncertain way of living, dictated so much by things out of our control, we had to be prepared for the unknowns that might be just beyond our present horizon. Those unexpected events that regularly demanded deep mental and physical reserves: illness, storms, broken equipment, sleepless nights or even a tight work deadline. Pacing myself wasn't just about getting to the end of a run now, but about always keeping enough in reserve to be fully engaged in every moment of every day.

*

The school half-term holidays in early June filled the campsite with the sounds of other families setting up their temporary holiday homes. The nights were noisy with over-excited sleepless kids, while evenings echoed with laughter, the sizzle of sausages and the clink of wine glasses.

In some ways it was good to have other families about. It allowed us to blend in rather than being the only people camping with young children as we had been for most of our trip so far. There was a big play area in the centre of the site, with a wooden obstacle course and plenty of mud and sticks to play with and, on the edge of the site, a shallow stream that all the kids played in. E was delighted at all the new company, and as ever we were happy to see her playing with children her own age. In other ways though, it brought an extra level of stress to our usually self-contained, peaceful existence.

One afternoon, after a disturbed and noisy night and a morning of short tempers all round, we had finally managed to get both kids to sleep. Without realising that I, too, had dozed off, I was suddenly awoken from a delightful, restful sleep by a loud chanting outside the tent.

'Come out and play! Come out and play!'

Some of the children E had befriended were standing right outside our tent door, demanding to see E who, along with Sim and H, was still sleeping peacefully. I lay still, silently wishing them away, longing to be allowed to just go back to sleep. But more chanting followed, and then a loud banging on the canvas. Eventually one unzipped the tent door and shouted in: 'E! We want you to come and play with us! Wake up!'

And then everyone was awake, E instantly enthusiastic about joining her friends, H crying loudly, and Sim and I feeling like joining him.

A few days later, the whole herd of children invaded our tent, stampeding over our possessions, our bedding, knocking things over as they went. I tried so hard to be relaxed and cheerful about it all, but unlike their own tents, which only needed to remain habitable for the week, this was our home. I found it hard to balance being happy that E had company with hating the invasion of our private space. I think Sim felt the same, but never as strongly as I did. He chatted easily with the other campers, while I hid inside our tent, wishing, and yet not wishing, that I was gregarious and easy-going too. I felt a pang of guilt at my inward celebrations when half-term was over and we had the place to ourselves once more.

*

Although it was now officially summer, the Cumbrian weather was still changeable, with regular rain, hail and strong winds coursing through the valley. We rigged up the tarp and cooked underneath it on our double gas hob, heating water for drinks in the Jetboil. The Frontier stove, too bulky and attention-seeking for cooking on outside at the campsite, would not come out again until we moved to the Welsh borders in July. There we would have far more space, no neighbours, and an easy supply of dry wood. But for now, our little kitchen offered safe and reliable cooking close to the tent.

Some mornings, the kids slept a little later giving Sim and I a bit of time together, just the two of us over coffee. Sitting close, breathing into the same patch of cold air, this was our time to talk, to plan, to write notes or to simply catch a moment of calm before the day properly began. It was time when we didn't need to worry about what E and H were doing, as we always did when they were up and about. I loved pulling on chunky walking socks, down jackets and woolly hats, enjoying the warmth they gave us until the sun rose high enough to cast its own warm rays into the valley. Then, suddenly unbearably hot, we stripped down to our summer clothes. From winter to summer in a few hours – it felt like the best of both worlds.

On the brighter June mornings, a male blackbird, neat in his black plumage and bright yellow beak, brought his fledgling along to feed on the abundant slugs that loitered under the damp leaves near to our tent. The baby bird was by far the larger of the two, fluffed up with speckled brown feathers, which camouflaged it in the sun-dappled undergrowth. It waited patiently nearby as its father chopped up the slugs carefully by scraping them on a stone with his beak, before taking them and popping them into the gaping, yellow-ringed mouth. We all loved this little scene, and as the days passed we became used to seeing them about, then expected it, looking forward to the moment when the two birds landed to share their breakfast at around the same time as we shared ours.

Those dry, sunny days we often climbed up into the fells with E and H, walking the steep, rocky path alongside Stickle Ghyll all the way up to Stickle Tarn, daring a quick swim below the stern, brooding gaze of Pavey Ark. Now that H was walking, he wanted to do so most of the time, protesting loudly when there was no option other than for him to be carried. This brought with it new joys – watching him toddling around the campsite, knowing it wouldn't be long before he would be running around after his big sister – but also new limitations as we needed to adapt our walks to suit his toddler legs, or head off while he was asleep in his sling. E seemed to be finding her mountain legs too, climbing most of the way herself and then paddling happily in the cold shallows. We took lunch with us, sitting in the sheltered combe with the Pikes rising above us and the ghyll tumbling down the fellside the way we had come, disappearing into the distant valley, far below. We climbed many of the higher tops around Langdale in those weeks. We were always making micro-decisions, judging safety, changes in the weather and how much we could expect the kids to cope with, trying to assess their limits – and our own.

One day we had set out for a walk with the kids asleep in their slings, aiming for Three Tarns which lies at the watershed of Great Langdale, in the shadow of the eastern side of Scafell. I'd run a hard eight miles in the morning and this was going to be another six or so, over very rough terrain, but I thought we'd take it slowly and it would be fine. The lower slopes were tough going, and I almost suggested to Sim that we should turn back and try this walk again on fresh legs in the morning, but instead I switched off the nagging voice of uncertainty. Of course it would be fine. After an hour or so of steady ascent, as we were climbing up a narrow, winding track above Hell's Ghyll, H began to wake up, fretting to be free of the sling. The track edged a steep gully that plummeted down the mountainside. The path itself was good enough, but a misplaced step to the right would send us skidding down the steep scree slope, literally into the jaws of Hell.

For a while I was able to keep the fear down, focusing on the non-precipitous side of the path, pretending the gaping void that with one stumble would swallow my baby and me didn't exist. I rationalised there was no reason to step off the edge of the path. If I was on the same path without H, or down there in the valley I'd have no trouble not stepping off it. But as we approached a particularly eroded section with boulders that I needed to scramble over, I froze and couldn't control the rising fear any longer. I've never suffered from vertigo or much in the way of fear in exposed and precarious situations, but this was different. H had started wriggling and, with him and a rucksack on, I was top-heavy and much less sure of my balance than usual. Suddenly it all felt very serious and an unnecessary level of risk. I stopped and sank down onto a boulder.

'Sim – wait!' I called ahead to where Sim was sauntering along with E on his back as if they were strolling along a pavement.

I shut my eyes, blocking it all out, trying to pretend none of it – the steep slopes, the glowering rocky summits, the endless suck of gravity – existed. I focused on slowing my breathing, slowing my heart rate, sinking down, down into the reassuringly solid earth. I know from years of experience how counterproductive panic can be in any potentially dangerous situation. The loss of control – both physical and psychological – that happens when we're deeply frightened can only ever make things worse. Many times before, on rock faces, long solo runs, open water swims and in remote places I have noticed, recognised and controlled this swelling of emotions, fighting it with logic and rationality in order to keep myself and those around me safe. I had to do the same now.

When I opened my eyes, Sim was standing in front of me looking surprised and concerned. 'What's up?' He crouched down so his eyes were level with mine, bringing E's little face down too, which now peered at me quizzically from over his shoulder.

'I don't know. I just . . . suddenly couldn't carry on. This path . . . it's too narrow and too steep with H jumping about. I'm OK. I just need a minute.' I looked at Sim, feeling pathetic, but also relieved to be feeling less anxious.

Sim sat down on a rock next to me, E perched happily on his back, and put an arm around me. 'Take as much time as you need. There's totally no rush. We can just turn around here if you like – we've come a good way up already.' He pulled a bottle of water out of the rucksack and handed it to me, following it up with a packet of jelly snakes, which we kept stashed in a secret zipped pocket, strictly for emergencies. E's eyes lit up. 'Jelly snakes!' she said, filled with her trademark contagious enthusiasm. Smiling despite myself I agreed they seemed an excellent idea.

There was no option but to head back down, H now as desperate to get out and walk as I was to stop him from doing so. But as soon as I stood up again, the vertigo slammed back into me, making me dizzy and unsteady on my feet. In the end, with a mixture of some pretty ungraceful bum-sliding, which fortunately kept H entertained, making him chuckle each time we hit a particularly large bump, I made it back to the end of the narrow section of path. In an instant, all my fears evaporated. It was a big lesson in where my limits lie when I'm with the kids, compared with when I'm on my own. In our constantly shifting demands and capabilities as a unit of four. In the need to acknowledge – to myself as well as to Sim – my concerns earlier on when we're out together, rather than silencing them, as I'd been used to doing when I was out alone.

*

With no mobile signal or WiFi at the campsite we needed to make regular trips into local towns to work. I was on my second coffee in the cosy back room of the Apple Pie Café in Ambleside, looking through the previous day's photos taken on a trip to pretty Loughrigg Tarn.

It had been a day of perfect light, which made the colours of the landscape sing. I'd never seen such blue sky, which, complete with almost cartoonishly fluffy white clouds, shone back from the mirror-flat surface of the tarn, balancing the images beautifully. The grassy valley floor was an almost luminous green, dotted with its own clouds of sheep. I'd been taking the photos, while the kids happily clambered around a big log just out of shot. I framed Sim as he ran, vibrant in a bright orange top, which now I looked at the pictures, popped out against the green exactly as I had hoped it would.

As I carefully judged each photo, discarding those I wasn't happy with, trying a different crop on some, marking others as being particularly pleasing, an email notification popped up. It was from the Official Receiver at the court that had been dealing with our bankruptcy case. I opened it and started to read.

' . . . *We have referred this matter for technical guidance, and I must inform you that the copyright to your book constitutes an asset in the bankruptcy estate, and therefore any royalties arising will be payable to the Official Receiver.*'

A wave of shock washed over me. I felt cold and sick. I read the email again, making sure I had really understood what they were saying: they were going to take our copyright away from us. The copyright that was our main source of income. How could they let us keep our other assets – the truck, the laptop and the camera – because these were necessary for our work, and yet take away our copyright?

I rang Sim, who was at the park with the kids.

'We need to talk. We've just had an email about . . . about . . .' *Bankruptcy.*

I didn't even want to say the word, not in public, not with the weight of judgement and stigma that still accompanies it. But we weren't the only ones – not by a long way. In the UK more than 300 people are declared bankrupt *every day* – that's one every five minutes. UK adults owe an average of £3,690 each in unsecured debt and, as a nation, we pay over £120 million per day in interest. Unmanageable debt and resulting financial vulnerability are growing, escalating problems affecting millions – 12 million people in the UK as I write. Yet I could hardly say the word to myself, much less admit it to anyone else.

Bankruptcy was supposed to set us free from our crippling debts. And yet, months later, it was threatening to make us worse off, both now and in the future. The royalties from our book made up about half of our income. Without it we simply didn't have enough to live on. If we couldn't sustain this way of life then what did we have? A tent but nowhere to pitch it. Work but nowhere to do it. And, though work was coming in, would people still want us if we no longer had a book to our names? I couldn't believe that all those years of work to secure our future could be wiped out.

We had tried so hard. First, to find a way to stay solvent, then to work our way through insolvency in the hope of building ourselves a secure footing. We had thought – had been told – that our case had been resolved and that we were free to move on. And yet here it was, rearing its horrible, ugly head once more. The injustice of it all lit a fire deep within me.

No. *No.* This was not going to happen.

*

Despite this new unpleasant turn of events, I found I was starting to enjoy having more people around – growing used to the busy sounds, friendly conversations with other campers and more regular company for E. On dry days, she spent most of her time out with the other kids, splashing in the shallow stream that ran through the site, playing hide-and-seek between the trees or joining other families for snacks and stories. It felt like we were part of an ever-changing yet like-minded community.

It also freed me up to spend time researching and putting together a case against the court's decision to take our copyright. But, without the means to pay for legal representation, we were far from sure we would be successful. I confided in a friend who set up a phone call with a lawyer friend who'd agreed to speak to us for free. The lawyer listened carefully as I ran through the details and then gave me instructions on putting together a clear and organised approach to our case. I thanked her as we said goodbye but couldn't really convey how much her contribution meant to us. It was yet another example of the kindnesses we experienced during our wild year.

The court had also contacted our publishers, who were incredibly understanding and agreed to support us through the process. I was so grateful to them but also felt so much shame at having to involve them in our financial mess. Eventually, after many revisions and difficult conversations, we posted off the letter that would, one way or the other, determine our future. For the next two weeks everything hung in the balance: our trip, our fledgling business, the hopes and dreams we had spent the past months nurturing.

Meanwhile, there was the immediate concern that our next royalty payment, on which we had been counting, had been seized by the official receiver. Suddenly, there wasn't enough in our bank account to cover the £3.99 monthly payment for our website and the site was taken offline. Lovely Sarah, realising what had happened, offered to pay it until we could pay her back.

*

At the end of June, having still heard nothing from the court, we moved to Eskdale in the south-west corner of the Lake District National Park. Here, the pebbly shallows of the River Esk held many shady spots for paddling with the kids and deeper pools for swimming. H loved to hold his hand in the clear, cold water and feel its pressure against him, watching the play of light and shadow between the shiny, dimpled surface and the dappled gold of the pebbles below. I found these moments of immersion – both in the cold, fast-flowing river and in the intricate, deeply imaginative world of the children – brought huge respite from our financial worries.

We made the most of the long, light, sunny days, playing in the water or following the gorse-lined riverside trail along the

Esk to Doctor Bridge and back over the rough, higher ground to the north of the river. We walked up into the fells to find Eel Tarn and Blea Tarn, sliding into the dark water that felt like iced silk on our skin.

The campsite was quiet and there was a picnic table near to our pitch, so on warmer days we could cook, eat and work outside. There was even a small play area with a trampoline, which kept the kids happy for hours. Eskdale was not as classically picturesque as other places we had visited in the lakes but it was a beautiful, wildly peaceful place to be. We seemed to intrigue the campsite staff, and they asked many questions whenever we ventured over to the tiny on-site shop. On one occasion, I had just finished showering when I overhead two of the cleaners discussing us and our year-long family camping trip. It was almost a comedy moment as I turned off the shower, plunging the building into silence just as the words, spoken loudly over the sound of the water, echoed around the concrete walls:

'Camping?! For a year?! With a baby?!'

I wondered how much either of the children would remember about their year in a tent. For H, perhaps nothing, E certainly very little. And yet I felt sure these experiences would become a part of them, influencing them in unconscious ways later on in life.

As we shouldered our adult concerns, watching our children experiencing all these new places, interacting with new people, feeling new sensations, living every moment with us in this intensely shared and sharing way, I couldn't shake my belief that it felt like a good thing to be doing for all of us.

*

It was the summer solstice and a beautiful evening, a mackerel sky, deep blue, scattered with pink-tinged fine weather clouds. I took E out to forage leaves – nettles, dandelions and the hairy bittercress that grew everywhere and tasted like watercress. I made these into soup, along with some garlic and our last potato. All together it made a fine *caldo verde*, although sadly without the *chouriço*.

After supper and getting E and H ready for bed, Sim and I settled into the open door of the tent just as the furthest edges of the sky beyond the rocky tops of the hills began to fade to indigo. Wrapped up warm against the chill of the evening breeze that whispered across the mountains, we saw out the longest day together. We had been in the Lakes for a little over a month and we were only just starting to feel we had experienced even a fraction of its incredible diversity. With our nights spent with our heads on the ground, ears to the earth and days filled with gushing becks, tumbling ghylls, steep-sided fells and rugged tops, it had felt like the lines between us and our surroundings were blurring; as if we were becoming part of each other. We had come here to seek out bigger landscapes – higher mountains, deeper lakes and extremes of weather – and we had found all these, and so much more.

That magical solstice night saw the calm and sunny break in the weather come to an abrupt end. The next morning was overcast, the sky a steely grey. Dark, tattered clouds hung in the distance, building, promising rain to come. We checked the forecast, which predicted gale-force winds and flood warnings for the coming week and decided to put the bell tent down while it was still dry. We could manage in our backpacking tent for the two nights before we left for a week in Yorkshire.

Our last night in Cumbria was filled with the big sounds of mountain weather. Deep into the darkest hours I awoke suddenly, instantly and intensely alert. As I lay listening, unmoving, feeling like a point of stillness amid the building storm, I could hear the wind gradually rising in volume. Every few minutes, I felt my body flinch involuntarily as the tent shook with the force of a gust, rattling the pegs, whining through the guy lines, a rapid crescendo that disappeared as suddenly to nothing. Then, from far away, softly at first, I heard a drumming, a rapid patter like a thousand hooves galloping up the valley. Fascinated, I realised it was a hailstorm approaching from a distant place. It hadn't reached us yet, our tent still dry as it sighed and heaved as if breathing in the wind. Sim and the kids still slept – but not for much longer, I thought, feeling adrenaline flowing through my body as I listened to the building volume, nearer and nearer, louder and louder, hammering across the fells. Then it was upon us, hitting the tent with the full force of its icy blast, roaring through the night in its ferocity. Everyone was awake now, sleep-addled minds trying to make sense of the sound and fury.

'Shhh.' I cuddled them close. 'It's OK. It's just the weather. It'll soon be on its way.'

The children were soon asleep again. They never seemed afraid of the weather. As long as Sim and I were there they were happy that all was well – they were safe and secure. Sometimes I wished it could always be this way, that I could shield them from every bad thing that would ever happen in their lives to come. But I also knew that they had to – and would want to – forge their own paths before long. Within minutes, just as suddenly as it had arrived, the storm was gone, moving on with the wind.

We could hear it beating its rhythm into the distance, booming through the cavernous glacial valley, the slippage route of so much more massive ice long ago.

We awoke to a morning that was grey and soft and still, as if the weather had simply tired itself out. While Sim packed the last remnants of our stay into the truck, along with the kids, I wandered over to the campsite reception in search of WiFi to check our emails. My heart started to race as I spotted one from the Official Receiver at the court, all the way back in Devon. I opened it and stood for several long, agonising moments waiting for the page to load. Eventually, the answer appeared on the screen.

They had read and considered our case and a decision had been made. The copyright would be returned to us. We had lost that six months' worth of royalties, and how we would manage without them we would have to figure out, but those payable in the future would be ours. Our precious book was ours. It had been close, and we could easily have given up, but I was so glad we had decided to fight. Not just for the rights to our book, but the right to carry on living this life we had chosen.

Idyll

Summer days in the Welsh borders

I HADN'T REALISED, UNTIL IT was lifted, how heavy the weight of anxiety had been. The anxiety of not knowing whether we would be able to continue with our wild year – and, if not, what then?

As we wound our way south through the Howgill Fells and into the Yorkshire Dales, I felt light, free, exhilarated with possibility. It was a feeling that stayed with me for the whole of our week in the Dales.

We had booked onto a campsite near to the village of Malham. Aiming not to need the car until we headed to the Welsh borders a week later, we stocked up on provisions in the nearby town of Settle, then wound our way up into the fells to find our campsite. It was a peaceful place, in the lee of a valley with a shallow stream and just a few tents dotted about among the trees. Sheep cropped the grass, chewing as they watched us unpack. All around rose an intriguing limestone landscape that we couldn't wait to explore.

During the day there were plenty of people about, walking on the Pennine Way and visiting the geological features for which the area is famous, but during the long, light mornings and evenings we had the fells to ourselves. That week we scrambled up the deep crevice of Goredale Scar, carved out of the rock by glacial meltwater; stood in awe before the vast scoop of Malham Cove; watched the delicate white veil of the waterfall at Janet's Foss; and boulder-hopped across Malham's extraordinary limestone pavement. The rock here is Great Scar Limestone, sculpted by the persistence of ancient rivers, waterfalls and seas, but formed 350 million years ago, when rising sea levels flooded northern England with warm, tropical waters. Sim studied geology at university, partly to spend as much time as possible rock climbing, but also because he wanted to know how the mountains he loved had come into being, and how such massive forces have shaped the landscapes around us. Through his knowledge I had come to see places anew, finding delight in knowing the difference between a valley formed by a river and one carved by a glacier; in understanding a little more about what lay beneath our feet and the ceaseless flow of heat and matter. Like learning to name the plants and creatures that inhabited our world, this small amount of extra knowledge added many layers of richness and detail to my experience of places. And, like all such things, made me yearn to know more.

One evening, long after the last visitors had left, we sat high up on Malham pavement. The long, dry valley stretched away into the hazy distance. The sun spilled luminous red-gold over the higher fells to the west. Like gazing into the impossible depths of a star-speckled sky, I found the connection with deep time that placing a hand upon these ancient rocks forged was dizzying, perspective-inducing, fathomless. Feeling the earth's vast history and my utter insignificance within it – what philosopher Albert Camus termed 'the gentle indifference of the world' – can be, when looked at in a certain way, almost comforting.

I watched E hopping from one slab to the next, investigating the tiny life forms in the worlds between them, pointing out crawling insects, feeling the soft greenness of moss. The grassy fellsides danced with wildflowers, and these were a particular delight to her. We found savoury-scented wild thyme; bright yellow buttercup, mouse-ear hawkweed, rock-rose and bird's-foot trefoil; the tiny white stars of fairy flax; the deep purple of mountain pansy, and the paler small scabious, alive with bees.

The days were warm and mostly dry, but some nights were surprisingly windy, heaving at the tent as we lay watching by the pale silver light of the summer moon. Each morning we checked the pegs, pushing them back in, and each evening we put away the tarp so it didn't flap about noisily during the night. At dusk, before the wind picked up, huge roosts of bats emerged from the nearby barns and swooped about, bug-hunting.

Running took us out along nearby stretches of the Pennine Way, south through fields walled with drystone alongside the meanders of the River Aire; north up the dry valley of Ing Scar; around the peaceful shores of Malham Tarn; and out across the bleak moorland of Fountains Fell.

Our time in the Dales was short but incredibly sweet. On the final day we packed up early and drove to Horton in Ribblesdale, walking with the kids to the summit of Pen y Ghent for breakfast then joining the motorway south towards our summer pitch in the Welsh borders.

*

I had grown up near to where we would be staying and a family friend had offered us the use of their field for nearly two whole months in return for gardening and keeping an eye on their house. It was a stroke of luck, allowing us to escape the hubbub and expense of summer campsites, and even more essential now our budget was so much less than we had expected. I couldn't wait to settle down for a longer spell, to have somewhere really all to ourselves – not like the abandoned loneliness of winter campsites but in a way that would mean we could really embrace this slow, outdoor way of life to its fullest.

As we reached the top of the hill from where a tiny, steep lane ran down to the field, we stopped for a moment, taking in the views across to the skyline to the west and the long spine of the Black Mountains, from Hay Bluff to Skirrid, sloping steeply at either end. Edging the eastern boundary of the Brecon Beacons National Park, the Black Mountains run along the border of Wales and England. They are lower and less dramatic and desolate than some of the better-known areas of the Beacons, such as its highest point, Pen y Fan. But for E and H, still growing their mountain legs, they would be a perfect introduction.

We followed the lane steeply downwards to a narrow

gateway at the entrance to the field. There we left the truck and made our way along a hedge-lined track, E running ahead in excitement, H still sleepy in my arms after the long drive, blinking in the bright daylight. We walked through an orchard of apple, pear and damson trees, and then out into an open area of rough grass. Sheltered by high, tangled hedges, the field was an approximate square, with a pond at one end and a sloping terrace at the other. As we walked its boundary, perambulating, searching for the flattest place to pitch the tent, I could already feel us all relaxing into the place. We could still hardly believe our good fortune in having this peaceful patch all to ourselves for the summer. Weeks and weeks with no need to pack up and move on – and no need to hunt for the nearest laundrette, either. A short walk from the field, we had the use of a toilet, shower and washing machine in a utility room separate from the main house. In return for all of this, we would keep an eye on the house, bring in the post each morning, and keep the garden tidy while its owners were away.

Travelling and camping with two young children there is always something: smoke, gravel, chemical spraying, rowdy neighbours, cars, dogs . . . Many times I found myself longing for the ability to make my body into a protective bubble around E and H, shielding them from these uncaring, unthinking purveyors of danger, sucking it all up into myself to keep my children from harm. But here, there was none of that, and I felt the tension of having spent so long on this mode of high alert dissipate into the quiet air. It was as if a persistent background noise had suddenly stopped and I hadn't even been fully aware of its existence until it was no longer there.

Our new home was also wonderfully private – privacy being another thing I now realised I had been longing for without consciously realising it. For the first time since we had set out, we would be free to enjoy the simple rhythm of our daily life under canvas, unobserved and unheard by anyone else. It is a strange thing, being on campsites so much, with such a thin layer of fabric between life inside and those outside. Every word, every sound, has the potential to be overheard. The everyday ebb and flow of emotions out there for all to witness. While, for the most part, I enjoyed the many and varied human interactions our itinerant existence gave us, it was also a relief to escape to our own private world for a few weeks.

With nearly two months in one place ahead of us, we set up the tent particularly carefully, smoothing every last wrinkle from our carpet and rug and arranging our duffle bags and boxes around the edges to give us a spacious living space in the centre. We pitched our backpacking tent next to the bell tent to give us separate living and sleeping quarters and strung the tarp between the two creating a large, undercover area. We hung our solar shower – a black bag with holes at the bottom that soaked up the sun's heat all day long – in the branches of a willow tree, whose slender cascade of branches formed a secluded, leafy bower. It was an utterly delightful experience to stand naked in the golden evening sunshine, bare feet on the warm mud, washing the day's dust and sweat away.

On one side of the field was an old apple tree, heavy with unripe fruit. It looked as though, at some point in its long life, it had simply grown tired and laid its gnarled trunk along the earth to rest. Its leafy branches now grew upwards and outwards from what was once the top of the trunk, spreading out like a parasol. E and H spent hours beneath its shady canopy, playing with the miniature unripe apples that lay in the earth or sitting on the horizontal trunk, which made a seat the perfect height for a child. We watched the steadily swelling bounty hanging tantalisingly from the fruit trees with envy, for all of it would remain stubbornly inedible until well after we had left.

The mornings were warm now, the heat waking us even before the light. Instead of porridge, we often had our oats simply soaked overnight in fruit juice and water, topped with nuts and berries. Those mornings smelled so delicious as the deeply mellow notes of freshly crushed coffee beans mingled with those of wet grass and the roses from the garden. In the long, light evenings we cooked on the Frontier stove, which now stood outside, a good distance from the tent, a thin plume of scented woodsmoke rising from its slender chimney. After supper, as the heat of the day faded, we ambled about the field with E and H until it was their bedtime. Then Sim and I would sit until darkness, enjoying the stove's residual warmth, listening to the birds' evening songs and watching fluttering moths, drawn to the light from our lantern.

The necessary simplifications of camp cookery – no oven, no fridge and limited storage space – and the various, evolving and strongly worded preferences of three-year-old E, meant that keeping meals interesting and engaging was a challenge. After a shop we made the most of having fresh produce while it lasted, then tapered off until we restocked again. In those warm summer months, we could only buy what we knew we would use before it spoiled, so we had to be inventive. The little milk we did use was UHT; cheese needed to be the hard, acidic type, like cheddar and parmesan; meat was almost non-existent, limited to the occasional pan of sausages cooked outside over the open flame of the stove. Bagged salad lasted a day, lettuce perhaps two, but root vegetables could easily last well for a week or more, particularly if we were able to keep them cool and dry.

Our new stability meant we could be a little more adventurous with cooking. When E was a baby, I was pleasantly surprised when she showed enthusiasm for one of my staple dishes – rice and dal. And now, though he hadn't been sure at first, H was a fan, too. It became a regular for us, cooked on the stovetop, boiling lentils in a big pan with stock, turmeric, garlic and ginger for gentle spice and sunshine. Sometimes I cooked a simple vegetable curry to go alongside, with foraged greens, spices, and whatever else we had available in a separate pan over the hot flame of a small camping stove, serving it all with fluffy basmati rice. Sitting around our little table, out on the dry grass or in the shelter of the tarp, this always felt like the happiest of meals.

It reminded me of growing up with my mum's cooking. When I was young, we lived in a diverse part of north London, with neighbours from all over the world. My mum would get them to teach her their favourite dishes, which she then tried out on us. We rarely went abroad, but this felt like travelling, each meal taking us somewhere different. My dolmades aren't a patch on Mum's, but I hope I can pass onto E and H something of that passion for different flavours. This was one of the many reasons I loved foraging with the kids – taking them to the woods and hedgerows to find free and delicious things to eat, creating those essential connections between our food and where it comes from. Often, they rejected salad when it was served up in a bowl at mealtimes yet would happily nibble on leaves of dandelion and bittercress when we were out picking it.

While living in wild places gave us such easy access to wild things, it also allowed them easy access to us. Crane flies dangled around the tent roof, their gauzy wings and long legs making fluttering, clicking sounds in the darkness; occasionally they would land on our faces in the night – a truly horrible sensation. Wasps joined our mealtimes, buzzing over our plates or landing on a forkful of food midway between plate and mouth. Mosquitoes feasted on me, in particular – I was glad, at least, that they seemed to avoid the kids – and I was left with huge, red welts that itched until they burned. But I noticed how quickly we all became used to sharing our lives with these creatures, until they became an essential part of the fabric of life. From the chorus of buzzing, humming insects on warm afternoons to regular visits from butterflies and songbirds, our interactions with the life around us were points of excitement throughout each day. How empty and alone we would feel without them.

The pond was a great source of entertainment. Both E and H loved to stand right at the very edge, fascinated by the watery world beyond, leaning out as we clung onto their tiny, sweaty hands. There was so much to see. Water boatmen sculled across the surface, their tiny feet dimpling the reflections. Dark masses of wriggling tadpoles hugged the edges, nibbling our hands when we dipped them into the water. Dragonflies rattled, loud and startling, overhead. Red and blue damselflies hovered and flitted and curled themselves around each other. In places, the surface of the pond was so covered in weed that it was hard to tell it was water. On one afternoon, as I sat outside the tent with H asleep in my arms, I watched a young black cat run straight onto the densely green weedy water, mistaking it for solid ground. Flailing wildly, it made it to the far side where it scrambled up the bank, glared at me furiously and disappeared, dripping, through the hedge.

In-between getting to know our immediate surroundings, we explored the local area, mapping it out in our minds as we looped the lanes and fields within easy walking distance. I found it interesting how we used our collection of paper maps to locate ourselves in each place – perhaps choosing a campsite because of its proximity to interesting features. But we rarely took a map with us when we went exploring, instead gradually building up our mental versions, learning how each crossroads and turning *felt*.

It was a two-mile walk to the top of the nearest hill, climbing steadily through a mixed woodland of oak, ash, sweet chestnut, birch and beech. These woods were a perfect place to ramble, cut through with wide, grassy rides, a dense leafy canopy sheltering us from both rain and sun. At the very top was an ancient hill fort, its ditches and ramparts still clearly cut into the earth more than two thousand years after it was first built. We could see why Iron Age humans had chosen the place, with its beautiful far-reaching views out across the valley. Sometimes it took us hours so make our small loop to the fort and back, as E and H searched the woods for food. There were wild raspberries to be found around every corner, hidden like tiny, bright rubies in an emerald jumble. Then there were bilberries, the occasional early blackberry, often tantalisingly out of reach, and even fat, red gooseberries, hairy and strange to touch but bursting with flavour. Berries were top of the list of the kids' favourite foods, but expensive to buy, so we made the most of having them freely available. Those woods nurtured us, generously providing us with food, shelter and entertainment, lifting our moods, filling our senses with its tastes, smells, sights and sounds.

Each day, as I reached the top of the hill on my run, I found the lure of the Black Mountains hard to ignore. We couldn't wait to explore them, but the weather was unpredictable, alternating hot sun with heavy rain and thunderstorms. Dark clouds tinged with pink glowered on the horizon, rumbling ominously. We couldn't risk being caught in a heavy downpour or electrical storm with E and H at the top of a mountain – so we waited, enjoying the simplicity of life at the tent. I grew up with distant views of these mountains, feeling them calling me to them across the wide stretch of the Golden Valley. I remembered walking there with my dad and the dog, long days riding hairy Welsh mountain ponies from the local stables, flying a kite I'd made at school. It was good to come back with my own family.

Over those weeks, carefully choosing the driest days, we walked up each of the nearby hills. First climbing the wooded flanks of Skirrid, emerging onto the long, rising ridge that leads to the summit, airy as a high mountain and yet walkable even for H. As we gazed down at the valley below, swirling with a misty cloud inversion, I told E and H about the legends surrounding the hill: how some people thought its distinctive shape, which gives it its name – Ysgyryd, in Welsh, meaning trembling or shaking – was caused by an argument between the Devil and Jack O'Kent. Others called it Holy Mountain, claiming it had split in two when Jesus died. While others still – particularly geologists like Sim – suggested it was to do with landslips.

A few days later, we climbed Sugar Loaf, starting high – even the car park has glorious views – and following one of the many gently rising trails of bright, sheep-cropped grass carving through dense swathes of bracken. H was walking a little further each time we were out, excitement carrying him along like wind in a sail, until he would suddenly stop and turn around, arms raised to be picked up. The path steepened towards the summit and we helped E make the final scramble up to the trig point. Sometimes I think young children don't appreciate views – being much more excited by what is immediately before them, but E was as captivated as we were by those from the top of Sugar Loaf. Out across the central Beacons to the table-top summit of Pen y Fan, to the shimmering ribbon of the Bristol Channel and even to the Cotswolds, which, as I tried to make them out through the summer haze, I realised with an unexpected pang of longing that I still thought of as home.

Our final walk was up Hay Bluff, the right-hand corner of the skyline as we looked at it. When we reached the top, it was more of a ridgeline than a summit – the Hatterall Ridge, which divides England and Wales along the line of the Offa's Dyke path, reaching Llanthony Priory in the Vale of Ewyas at its southern end. We had considered walking the ridge, to see how far we could get. But when we reached it, the whole plateau around the top of Hay Bluff was a dense carpet of bilberries, and we got no further, losing the children to their sweet-sharp allure – and not minding in the slightest.

In-between ticking off this inviting skyline, we enjoyed the peaceful privacy of our field. When the weather was good there was little need to go anywhere else. The kids were daily absorbed in the tiny worlds to be found under stones and wooden planks, peering in at woodlice, earthworms and ants, disturbing a family of voles beneath a sheet of corrugated metal, and following the tiny frogs that hopped through the wet grass near the pond. Keeping young children entertained can be such hard work, but sometimes it can also be delightfully easy.

As July drew to a close, the weather seemed to get hotter by the day. No longer were mornings and evenings a cool respite from the heat. It was as if it had saturated everything – trees, rocks, buildings, the earth we slept upon – all radiated the sun's energy long after dark. It became too hot to sleep in our backpacking tent – even with all the vents open the tiny airspace was stifling. We tried leaving the door unzipped, but the whine of mosquitoes soon made us zip it back up again. We moved our beds into the bell tent, which, with its single layer of fabric and better airflow, was far cooler and at last we had some more comfortable nights. On a trip to stock up on groceries we bought an inflatable paddling pool, which E and H spent hours in. Sometimes, after a run through the heat of the day, we'd jump in with them.

On those long summer days filled with the simple happiness of being together in this idyllic place, I found myself pointlessly wishing things could stay like this forever. I wished we didn't have to move on once September arrived, that we didn't have to step back into the world of campsite living and the endless packing and unpacking it entailed, that the future beyond our wild year was a little more settled.

There was also something casting a dark cloud over the coming weeks of our stay. Something that struck fear into my very being, set my heart racing and my nerves jangling every time I thought about them. *Festivals*.

Appearances
Festivals and retreat in the Welsh borders

THINKING BACK TO OUR very first festival appearance still makes a small part of my insides shrink into a tight ball of mortification. We had agreed to deliver a talk about trail running in Britain at the request of our publishers just a few weeks after *Wild Running* was published. Sim's parents had offered to look after the children while we spoke, allowing us to concentrate on presenting while knowing that they were in good hands. Leaving a sleeping H and an over-excited E with their grandparents, we made our way out onto the stage, bright lights shining in our eyes, an audience of vastly more experienced writers, photographers and adventurers gazing up expectantly at us.

We were so nervous. Thinking it would calm my nerves I had brought a prompt sheet, but soon lost my way and then had to search through in a panicked silence to find what I needed to say next. Sim ploughed valiantly on. Later, while Sim was showing a short film clip of a run along a beautiful mountain ridgeline, I popped backstage to check on the kids. I opened the door to find H screaming at full volume, Sim's poor mum walking laps of the room, a desperate look on her face, which instantly turned to relief when she saw me. I took H in my arms, his distress rendering me incapable of doing anything else. Unfortunately, I had forgotten to turn my microphone off, and so – I was told later on – the audience received the full blast of H's fury echoing in stereo around the auditorium. In the end, we finished our talk as we delivered all subsequent ones, with H in his sling on my front and E pottering about our feet. It became something of a family motto: all together or not at all.

This August, we had been invited to appear at a few different festivals to talk about our book and our wild year, and to lead guided runs. With festivals over two weekends, but neither more than a couple of hours' drive away, I resigned myself to simply getting through them. There were definitely some upsides: we met lots of lovely people, including families who were keen to chat about their own adventures, and big names from the outdoor world whose stories we were fascinated to hear. And we listened to some great live music – for as long as the kids were happy. But we found these festivals incredibly stressful.

We had got better at public speaking – I now know that I cope much better if I simply learn the whole thing by heart – but I still struggled with the idea of standing up and talking in front of people, and this was made so much harder by not having any childcare. If H slept through the talk, as he sometimes did, everything was fine. But if he decided he wanted to feed or play part-way through I wasn't sure how I'd manage. Sim is naturally more confident on stage, but like me found everything else that came with festival appearances difficult – partly the travel and the crowds; partly because to buy almost anything at a festival was far beyond our budget and partly because young children and drunk people aren't a terribly fun mix.

From hard-won experience, we knew how much a flat pitch could make or break a good night's sleep. But at festivals we were invariably pitched on a slope, and spent the night pushing the kids back up the hill in their low-friction sleeping bags. We arrived at one event a day later than most people, to find the only space left to pitch was sandwiched between a floodlight and a generator. People stumbled drunkenly past our tent all through the night, tripping over our guy lines, damaging our tent. We usually received no pay for these appearances, but attending two or three each year was a good opportunity to meet people and promote our book. Sometimes we would make some money selling books, of which we had a small stock packed carefully in a waterproof box in the back of the truck, direct to festival goers but often it was not enough to cover our fuel expenses.

Perhaps, if money hadn't been so tight, I could have relaxed a little and enjoyed the opportunity to attend these weekends for free. But being surrounded by crowds of happy people, eating, drinking and partying, when even the cost of a round of ice-creams was out of our reach was thoroughly depressing. It was an odd experience, being one of the acts – one of the attractions that brought people to festivals that often cost hundreds of pounds per ticket – and yet quite possibly being the poorest people there. Each time we would return, fractured by stress and sleep deprivation, desperate for the tranquillity of the field.

*

In contrast, summer was glorious and blazing in our peaceful meadow. The wider area within easy reach was particularly rich with rivers – the Wye, Monnow, Dore and Usk. There were numerous smaller streams and brooks, too, and I revelled in their delightful names as we looked over the map, spread out on our tent floor: Worm Brook, Garren Brook, The Gamber, Wriggles Brook, Wells Brook, alongside many unnamed others.

I have always loved the River Wye, which flows from Plynlimon – the highest point in the Cambrian Mountains of Mid Wales – to join the Severn Estuary at Chepstow. Tracing its looping course across the map brought back many memories from years ago, when I had spent long days riding a friend's ponies across farmland near Ross-on-Wye, gone kayaking and scrambling at Symonds Yat or gazed in awe as it took over fields and farmland in winter floods. More recently, before the kids arrived, Sim and I had spent some enjoyable days climbing esoteric routes up the crumbling cliffs of the Wye Valley.

During the first week of August we celebrated E's fourth birthday, a happy day with a picnic and paddling down by the river. There was a chocolate cake, shop-bought but decorated ourselves, with edible flowers and a toy pony. Having just turned four, E could start school in September – only a few weeks away now – but we had made the decision to delay this for a year. Even aside from the fact that we didn't have anywhere permanent to live, it felt like the right decision for all of us. Sim and I had lengthy discussions about school; we both felt E might find it easier being one of the oldest in her year, rather than one of the youngest. And we were happy to have the privilege of her full-time company for another year.

With so much all around us to keep E and H busy, our weeks in the Welsh borders were also a productive time for writing. There was good mobile signal at our field so, with an unlimited data contract, we had internet access at the tent and electricity via an extension lead from a nearby barn. We'd had the exciting news of a contract for our second guidebook, about family adventures in Britain, something we were certainly living on a daily basis. The advance from this had made up for the shortfall in income from our copyright and gave us some much-needed financial breathing space for the months to come. We had also agreed our first regular magazine work – a monthly running column in *Outdoor Fitness* magazine – which gave us another small but, importantly, regular source of income. Working for ourselves, pitching for new work, creating a sustainable income through a patchwork of different projects for different organisations was something we enjoyed but was never easy. It was sometimes nerve-wracking, not knowing what, if or when the next job might be. It kept our days varied and interesting, if a little stressful.

Our final fortnight in the Welsh borders was, if anything, even more idyllic than the earlier weeks now the stresses of festivals were behind us. Either Sim or I would head out to run before breakfast, taking a container with us to collect berries. I grew to love those early morning runs, finding I had the world to myself as I explored quiet country lanes, linked up footpaths across hedge-lined fields, followed old droving tracks or found new ways through the woods. During the day we wrote, walked across the field to the house and brought in the post, weeded or mowed the garden, repaired our kit and read, played or explored with the kids. In the hot sun of the afternoons, we hid in the cool shade of the woods. In the evenings, after supper, we walked a loop of the narrow lanes from the field, plundering the hedgerows as we went. Every stretch of hedge was heavy with shiny, ripe blackberries, and a walk of less than a mile could easily take us an hour or more. Browsing in this way took us to an almost meditative level of consciousness, connecting deeply with an ancient hunter-gatherer part of our being.

As much as we wished they could last forever, our days in the Welsh borders were coming to an end. Staying put in the meadow had reminded me of the deep joys of making a home – even a temporary tented one. Of being able to exhale, unobserved, in privacy. Of watching the seasons bring new things to a familiar place. We longed to linger as the damsons, apples and pears ripened on the trees. It made both of us dream of one day owning a little orchard of our own – a dream that, at that moment, felt very distant indeed.

Once again, we packed up our home, clearing the area of everything we had brought with us. It was a fair walk across the field and back to the gate, so it took a while to disassemble our camp and pack it all back into the truck. But, when it was done, we stood together in fond farewell to the place we had spent nearly two whole months of our wild year. The land looked very much as it had when we had arrived, just a little further on the season. There was a circle of flattened, yellowed grass where our bell tent had stood and, next to this, a rectangle that had been our backpacking tent. Apart from these signs, which would soon vanish as the light reached the grass once again, we would leave no trace of our time here. Yet it would leave a lasting mark on all of us.

AUTUMN

'All the months are crude experiments, out of which the perfect September is made'.

Virginia Woolf.

Turning

A return to Exmoor and Dartmoor

AFTER THE EXTREMES OF heat and storms of the summer months, September seemed more laid back; more relaxed, somehow, right from the outset. Through a landscape gilded with ripening crops, we wound our way south and then west to Exmoor, tracing the coastline along the edge of the Bristol Channel. The hills were so steep, rising and falling, echoing the cliffs and combes of the coast, that our heavily laden and ageing truck struggled with the gradient and tightness of the bends, skidding around tight corners, tyres skipping, a smell of over-heating clutch and brakes filling the air. I shut my eyes, refusing to let it in, hating the unnerving, slightly out-of-control sensations of steep hills, winding roads and precipitous drops. Sim's a good driver – careful, considerate and experienced – and he understands the source of my car-related fears. To his credit, he never complains about what a terrible passenger I am.

We were keen to explore more of the north coast of Exmoor and had chosen a quiet campsite on grassy banks of Badgworthy Water, an area that inspired R.D. Blackmore's novel, *Lorna Doone*. 'Through the dewy meadow's breast,' wrote Blackmore of this place, 'fringed with shade, but touched on one side with the sun-smile, ran the crystal water, curving in its brightness like diverted hope.'

We pitched our tent on the sun-smile side of the water, a flat, green expanse of valley floor, which once must have borne a much greater river. On the shady side opposite rose a dense wood of ancient, twisted oaks, lichen encrusted and hairy with moss, clinging to the steep slope of the valley. Higher still, to every side, rolled the empty reaches of Exmoor, purple and russet with heather.

Crossing the footbridge a little downstream from the tent brought us to a shallow, shingly area where we paddled, feeling the hard sharpness of the stones under our feet, the tickle of tiny fish swimming by. As we explored further along, we found a dead ewe, its eyes pecked out, lying right across the footpath. I urged the children on, rather than going up to have a better look, but they were more intrigued than upset.

When we returned to the campsite, I spotted the elderly farmer whose land it was and told him about the sheep. Rubbing his stubbly chin with a hand as gnarled as the twisted oaks across the valley, he shrugged. 'It's what it's like in the countryside love. Not like your towns here. It's . . .' he gestured vaguely at the hills, searching for a word that would help me understand, '. . . *wild*.'

For the brief and sunny time that we stayed, it was delightfully wild. The kids ambled around the cropped grass where brilliant, clear light filtered through mossy branches from a bright blue sky. Dragonflies and dippers visited the water, which rushed past our tent day and night. A tiny robin befriended us, perching on our guy lines which, at the time, were covered in several small items of clothing that we didn't want to risk tumble-drying. It even ventured inside both the tent and the truck when we left the doors open, searching for crumbs. H was beside himself with excitement every time it appeared. He loved to watch it, entranced by such a tiny, bold being, and the bird seemed to know, fixing H with its beady eye until he shared his breakfast. As we left the tent for the washrooms one morning we discovered a slow worm, cold and immobile, waiting for the sun to rise enough for its warmth to flood down into the valley. Very carefully, we picked it up and placed it into E's cupped hands. It made my heart leap with joy to see her face light up as her warmth brought the creature to life and it began to explore her sleeves.

While the days were still warm and bright, the Exmoor nights were surprisingly cold and dark, with a new moon and clear skies, a hint at the changing seasons to come. One night, I sat with E in the open door of the tent, both of us wrapped in warm, woollen blankets, tracing meteors and satellites across the vast blackness that arched over us. There was the bright silver glimmer of Venus, the first star to appear, and Mars with its reddish tint.

It brought back happy memories of stargazing with my dad when I was a child; the feeling of awe and otherness that I always felt looking up at such impossible vastness. I wandered through those memories: leafing through a big book with glow-in-the-dark constellations, trips to the planetarium and the

Science Museum in London, and once to Jodrell Bank to see the massive Lovell Telescope where my sister and I ate freeze-dried ice-cream like the astronauts had in space. I thought of some of the other things my dad had introduced me to that I still carried with me: long distance running, Ursula K. Le Guin, the poetry of Ted Hughes, a love of dogs and hens – and never doing what I was told.

Each day Sim and I ran long loops out over the surrounding hills, moors and coastline: west over Malmsmead to Shilstone Hill; north along Badgworthy Water, up the leg-sapping climb to County Gate, and down to the wooded combes of the South West Coast Path; east across the commons to Great Tom's Hill; and south over Trout Hill and Great Buscombe to Simonsbath.

We visited the local towns of Lynton and Lynmouth, taking a big bag of washing to the laundrette in Lynton. Waiting out the time it took to run through a cycle, we stumbled upon a tiny café – Charlie Friday's – where we were welcomed like old friends, despite never having been there before. The staff at Charlie Friday's seemed fascinated by our adventure and asked us question after question about our life under canvas. We've returned a few times since, enjoying its cheerful, colourful, friendly buzz and warm welcome.

During our visit to Exmoor, we were offered a couple of nights in a newly converted bothy – a former pigsty – at Peppercombe on the North Devon coast in return for writing about our stay. It was not far out of our way and sounded intriguing, so we accepted enthusiastically and drove west through Barnstable and Bideford, turning off the main road and following a rough track down into a wooded coastal valley.

The tiny, white-painted bothy was basic but clean and dry, and certainly an interesting change from camping. The best bit was the outdoor loo – a wooden shed attached to the back of the building from which stretched a glorious view out across the sparkling sea to the island of Lundy. One evening, popping out before bed, I was treated to a spectacular sunset, blazing red and gold across the western sky. Not even the most luxury hotel bathroom could have come close.

The bothy had running water but no electricity – it amused me that we scarcely noticed its absence after so long in the tent. Reached by a rough, half-mile-long track from the nearest road, there was no mobile signal anywhere nearby and just the owls, the deer and the distant hush of the sea for company.

We spent the two days of our stay exploring the untamed jungle of woodland and stretch of coastline from the door of the bothy. But we soon discovered that, after a warm, wet summer, the area of grass and trees around the bothy was alive with ticks. Aware of the risk of Lyme Disease, we were used to keeping an eye out for them and, whenever we explored places we knew they were likely to be – woods, moors, heaths and uplands – particularly over the warmer months, we were careful to check everyone thoroughly afterwards. But we had never seen so many before, finding them crawling over our shoes even after the short walk from the bothy to the truck. One afternoon, as H dozed on my lap, I noticed with horror a tick hidden in the soft baby folds of his thigh. We had a special tick removal tool with us and carefully pulled the vile creature out, taking care not to leave any of it embedded in H's skin. After that we had to check ourselves, each other and the kids almost constantly until we left the bothy. Our stay had been enjoyable, but it was a relief to return to the cropped grass of the campsite with its more pleasant varieties of wildlife. It was time, too, feeling the ebbing year calling us back to more familiar places, to pack up and make our way south to Dartmoor.

*

Wending our way along the familiar lanes, we found Dartmoor ablaze with autumn colours: deep greens and golds and purples of bracken and gorse and heather, vivid against a cloudless blue sky. Our first stop was at Sim's parents' house for a celebratory reunion supper – an evening of warmth and wine and being looked after that felt all the more special after several months away.

We went through the ritual picking up of post, sorting out kit and swapping the kids' books and toys around. Though it was only one evening, to sit on a comfortable sofa and, for a few hours, not fend for ourselves felt almost overwhelmingly good.

We had arranged to camp near to Tavistock, on the western edge of Dartmoor, a place of ancient stone circles, vast swathes of tussocky grassland and granite tor-topped hills. We were shown to a spacious corner, bordered on two sides by dense mixed hedges, speckled with colourful red campion and gently shaded by young oak and ash trees. Now the summer was at an end and there were fewer campers about, we were once again able to pitch both tents. They looked wonderfully homely nestled together beneath the hedge. We had brought with us a string of solar lights, each light a metal star, which we strung between the two tents. Their soft twinkling added a little magic to the evenings and were a useful guide when we returned to the tent in the dark.

The campsite had an end-of-season friendliness, and we had many interesting conversations during our stay. Nearest to us were a local postwoman, caravanning with her tiny dog, and a Dutch couple, touring Britain in a huge motor home with their young son. When E started complaining of pain from a new tooth that was coming through, and we discovered we had run out of Calpol, they offered us some infant paracetamol to tide us over until we could go to a chemist the following day. What we hadn't realised was that this commonly comes in the form of a suppository in the Netherlands, a suggestion met with blunt refusal by a horrified E.

One evening, walking up to the summit of the nearest tor, we heard a thundering of hooves behind us. We stopped and turned to see a herd of ponies charging over the brow of the hill, snorting, squealing and raising a cloud of dust behind them. Perhaps, like us, they could feel the pressure dropping, the tingle of electric excitement at the sense of a storm rising: dark clouds now sliced through with bright, midsummer sunlight but already gathering, ready for a full night of rain. We made it back before the first heavy raindrops began to fall, and had supper in the tent listening to the *pat-pat-pat* on the canvas.

That night, as I lay in the darkness listening to thunder rumbling and cracking across Dartmoor, I thought of all the storms we had weathered. I remembered how terrifying I had found them when we set out, when we didn't know if the tent would hold, when we were still so sensitive to every sound and sway that is a part of life under canvas. Now, though, I felt no fear. Instead I was enjoying its progress, its changing volume and pitch, knowing from becoming attuned to these sounds that it would soon be on its way.

The light evenings would not last much longer, so we decided to celebrate being back on Dartmoor with a wild camp. We walked straight from the campsite, leaving the bell tent pitched and taking only our backpacking tent and what we'd need for the night. The dipping sun painted the moor's high points bright gold, and made long, strange shadows of the stubby, wind-sculpted trees.

We had identified a possible site on the map before we had left, just over the tor that filled our immediate horizon and then a couple of miles down into a deep valley, edged by trees and with a small stream running through its centre. A little over an hour later we reached it. It was a breezy evening, which kept the midges away, even close to the stream, so we decided to camp on a wide circle of sheep-cropped grass, only a few steps from the water. We pitched the tent and spread out a blanket on the grass, then took E and H paddling, the sounds of splashing feet and excited voices mingling with the cronk of ravens and the mew of buzzards in the quiet evening air.

Later, Sim and I lay together on the blanket outside the tent in the darkness, a vast, black, moonless sky speckled with billions of stars stretching over us. E and H were asleep, snuggled into sleeping bags in the tent. It felt like the first moment we'd had together for such a long time.

'Have you thought about what we might do next?' Sim's thoughts, as mine, had turned to the passing autumn days, the end of our wild year, the coming of another winter and what that might bring.

'I don't think I can do another whole winter of camping,' I admitted. 'But I'm also not sure how we're going to manage to avoid it.'

Sim squeezed my hand. I could feel his warmth along the length of my side, comforting against the chill of the night. 'We'll work it out. We're all together, so we'll be fine.'

Sim rarely worries. He starts from a point where he assumes everything is going to be brilliant and, if it's not, he works on making it brilliant. I have spent my life spotting the potential problems ahead and working out how to avoid them. Not in a pessimistic way, but in a proactive way: I don't want to get caught out by the bad stuff or miss out on the good. Together, we have both the courage to try things and the foresight to avoid at least most of the pitfalls along the way.

There was no doubt we were closer to being able to afford to rent somewhere again. Somewhere in a place we wanted to be, where we would be more in control of our lives than we had been before, one of the purposes of embarking on this wild year. But we were not quite there yet. Our income was still too uncertain, still too variable.

I thought back over the past year. I had no regrets about our decision, and I knew Sim felt the same – quite the opposite as it had given us so much: experiences, freedom, time together, time to build back up from the rock bottom we'd hit a year earlier. But at the same time, it had taken everything we had, and sometimes more. It felt like we were coming to the final miles of a really long run and had paced ourselves, leaving just enough energy to get to the finish. The idea of another winter in the tent felt a bit like asking us to turn around and run all the way back again.

The next morning waking early to find sunshine streaming in through the canvas, I felt our impromptu night out on the moor had done its job, reconnecting us with the peaceful remoteness of wild places. As we packed the tent away, E and H spotted a common sexton beetle, its black and orange zigzags vivid against the grass. We watched the little creature as it wound its way through a maze of foliage and stones, eventually disappearing into a patch of heather. Then we sat on a large, flat boulder by the stream and had flapjacks and apples for breakfast.

Home Strait
The end of a wild year

MORE THAN EVER, NOW, I had started to think about home. What did 'home' mean to us all? Did it have to be a particular place – or could it just be about the people we were with? Or a feeling we carried around with us? I thought of how the homes we arrange around ourselves come to reflect who we are. We hang pictures on our walls, stand mementos on our shelves. We *decorate*. Even if we do none of these things that still says something about us. When I visit someone's house, I always notice their books first. Such a glimpse into the soul – a glossary of interests, political and religious leanings, passions and neuroses, right there, laid out along the shelves.

We had given up our house and yet, when we were all together in the bell tent, we still strongly felt that sense of being home. The tent carpet didn't match the tablecloth. We didn't have curtains – we didn't even have windows – and yet we felt surrounded, embraced, by a sense of belonging, of acceptance, of safety. For all its portable, temporary nature, the space created by poles and canvas that simply disappeared each time we packed it away always felt like our home.

Sim grew up in a house where people came and went daily – some friends, others strangers; some helping out, others needing help. He has a welcoming, open-house approach that I admire, yet also find difficult. My home, I now know, doesn't have to be a specific building or a particular place, but it does need to be my refuge. It is where I can be myself: private, separate from public. It took a year or so without what most people would consider a home to really understand what it means.

For many years I had sought the idea of home in so many of the wrong places. But now, without the faintest shadow of doubt, I knew I had found it, in these relationships with those closest to me. This feeling seemed to grow stronger each day, month, year we spent together, in the life we were – are – building together, and I will guard it for the rest of my life, for myself and my children, as fiercely as I know how.

*

With October's arrival on Dartmoor, it felt as though the year had turned firmly to autumn. There were many days of heavy, persistent rain that hammered on the canvas and the moors, bouncing off the hard granite boulders that dotted the rough grassland. Big splashing drops made muddy chocolate-brown puddles and sent the streams gushing and gurgling off the moor. In the tent, on days like these, I felt us drawing inwards, finishing all the things it was so hard to find time for when the sun shone. Sim and I worked hard, writing, editing, pitching, snatching moments of productivity while E and H slept or played. Sooner or later we would all venture out, driven by cabin fever, heading for streams and puddles and trying not to mind too much about the mud and wet seeping into everything, for it was all worth the joy on our children's faces.

Seeing many different wild places was one of the things I had looked forward to most when we set out on our camping year, but now I was starting to feel I'd had enough of moving around. If only for a while, I wanted to stop, to use our time more productively, frustrated by the need to pack and unpack every time we moved. But the weather forecast was so much better near the coast, so we decided to leave the wet and windy wilds of Dartmoor and head back to the South Hams, where we had enjoyed some of the early part of our year. The private field we had camped in back then was no longer available, but we found a campsite right near the sea at Slapton Ley, perfectly placed for the shingly crescents of Beesands, Slapton Sands and Blackpool Sands – places we had only been to in passing before.

Each day our pockets steadily filled with the stones that E and H collected from the beach. These, we were informed, were special treasure and could not be left behind. The rucksack was often noticeably heavier at the end of the day as we dragged it back up the hill to the tent. But we had learnt from our previous mistakes when, assuming that these precious sticks, pebbles, shells and pinecones would be forgotten by the time we got back to the tent and emptying them along the way, we had been met with fury and tears on the discovery they were gone.

One morning I ran the eight winding, undulating miles into Dartmouth as heavy fog rolled in, arranging to meet Sim and the kids later on in the town, the promise of a hot pasty for lunch beckoning. The conditions were strange, with brief moments of hot sun interspersing a rolling fog that soaked through my clothes and hair and obscured everything – hills, trees, sea, land.

Several times I had the feeling I was running without going anywhere, caught for eternity on a narrow stretch of coast path that wound forever through dense grey cloud. It felt a little like this year – a trail whose end point was still so far away that it vanished into the mist, too indistinct to strive for as an immediate goal. Instead, each and every moment required fully *being within*, doing what we could right here and now, and trusting it would work out in the long run.

*

As autumn took hold, it was exciting to see many different varieties of apples appearing in woods, hedgerows and orchards. Some were huge, others tiny; some shone bright green, others glowed deep red or sunshine yellow from within a dense tangle of branches. Many were unlike any apple we had seen or tasted before – the spectrum of scents and flavours was startling – how had our everyday apples become so much the same? A favourite discovery was the beautiful, pink speckled Killerton Sweet, whose original trees are found only on the Killerton estate in Devon. Apples were popular foraging for all of us and it was always exciting to try a new variety, although sometimes they turned out bitter and tannic and were swiftly returned to the hedgerow. We found many uses for the tastier fruit, stewing them up with cinnamon and raisins to add to pancakes or porridge, or slicing them into boats for E and H to dip into peanut butter.

As October drew on, we started to see flyers for Apple Day celebrations dotted about the South Hams. Held on or around 21 October each year, Apple Day was created in 1990 by charity Common Ground, co-founded by the late Roger Deakin. Its purpose is to reconnect communities with their natural environments and to treasure, in the founders' own words, 'Local Distinctiveness'. Apples come in so many varieties – more than 2,000 eaters and cookers plus hundreds more for cider – often specific to an area and an important part of the heritage of a place. Once, whole villages would have been heading for the orchards at this time of year.

On a sunny Saturday morning, we headed for the orchard, which was already busy with small groups of people and lively chatter. It was uplifting seeing so many families out together, exploring the local countryside, learning about apples and getting involved with harvesting. The trees stood heavily laden, bathed in the hazy light of autumn, the air filled with the fruity, alcoholic scent of those already decomposing, buzzing with wasps and crawling with earwigs in the grass. We joined in and wandered about picking, tasting and filling mesh bags with apples until they bulged voluptuously, lifting the kids high into the branches to pick those further up. Two waiting ponies saddled with a pair of buckets each carried the bags of apples down the hill to the waiting press. There they were rinsed and squashed, folded into big pieces of material and crushed under a heavy weight, extracting the clear, sweet juice which was then ready for tasting. It was better than any apple juice we had ever tried: sweet, fresh and fragrant. It was a joyful day, and a memorable way to experience and celebrate Local Distinctiveness. We left with full hearts and two bottles of the previous year's cider.

*

Autumn sounded different. High on Dartmoor, the wind clattered through drying leaves where until recently it would have whispered through soft foliage. Gone was the bright grass underfoot and in its place a deep, rustling, crunching sea of leaves. The light was different, too. Low-slung it lengthened shadows and gilded edges, tinting a soft-focus world. Low cloud hung damply over the moors on some days, giving everything a stealthy drenching. It's not like rain when you can stand under a boulder and stay dry; instead the air seems made up of suspended water droplets, to be gathered up as you pass through. By the time we had walked a mile it was everywhere, condensed, beading along our eyelashes and soaking into our boots.

It felt fitting that the end of our wild year coincided with the fading and darkening of the natural year. The need for rest and regeneration, and the desire to retreat to warmth and shelter, always such a feature of autumnal days, was strong. Under normal circumstances it's a feeling I love but, with warmth and shelter being so much more difficult than normal, it was tempered by worry this year about what was to come. Already we were being reminded of the harshness of living wild over the colder months, with long, dark evenings testing us. Even cooking our family meals felt more difficult now, when everything in the gloomy evenings just looked grey.

Our work plans were gradually taking shape for the months ahead and we were working hard on our new book about family adventures. We had managed to arrange a few press trips, for which accommodation for the four of us was provided. This was something we hadn't done before and it felt excitingly novel to be discussing itineraries with PR people. These trips would be both a great way to experience new places for our various writing commissions, and much-needed breaks in what looked to be a second winter of camping.

Back in Slapton, where the campsite would soon be closing for the winter, there were just a few other tents on the site, and some campervans, mostly older couples grabbing the last sunshine of the year. They were friendly, chatting with the children, and commenting on H's age. We nodded and smiled as we always did when they told us how young he was to be camping, and how brave we were to camp with such little ones. Little did they know.

E decided to put them straight.

'We've been camping for a WHOLE YEAR!'

'A whole year?' one of the women said indulgently, raising her eyebrows as she leant towards E. 'I expect it feels like that with all this rainy weather we've been having.' The group chuckled and the woman cast a knowing look in our direction. 'So lovely at this age, aren't they?'

*

A year ago, when we had made our final preparations to set out on our wild year, there had been so many unknowns, so many variables, yet also so much excitement and anticipation. Would we make it through the winter? Would we be able to make enough money to live on as we went? How would it all pan out? We had known there would be challenges along the way, but more than anything we couldn't wait to escape a life that had made us all so unhappy, so unsatisfied. The thought of spending all our time together, building our dream together, having fewer financial struggles felt worth any uncertainty to come.

Now we knew the reality, and we knew exactly what it had taken. We had relished the freedom and the choices our wilder life had given us. But we had also struggled with money and anxiety and the weather, battling through the storms that all three brought with draining regularity. We had overcome so many challenges by facing them together, but we had never really been alone. None of it would have been possible without the incredible kindness of others, from our families to the friends and strangers who noticed us, understood our position and stepped in to help.

Part of me dreaded relinquishing our freedom, the thought of returning to a house with rent and bills to pay. But we had also discovered there's a kind of freedom that comes with staying in one place – the ability to plan, to dedicate the time and space to work, to try, in our own small ways, to shape the world we want our kids to grow up in. We missed having a community, friends and a garden . . . We missed having somewhere of our own to nurture, and that could nurture us in turn.

As we entered the final week of our wild year, it was hard to believe it was nearly over. Although little would actually change once October turned to November, as we passed the arbitrary end point of our self-imposed challenge, we knew it would *feel* different. We were facing another winter under canvas, which this time wasn't a thought I relished, but I knew we had it in us. We had done it before; we could do it again. I tried to remember and hold on to all the things about our wild year that I would miss once we lived more normally again: the joyful simplicity of daily life; the utter immersion, day and night, in nature; the ability to slow down, to notice and to fully appreciate the world around us. Even when we did have four walls and a roof again, I would try to make sure we never gave those things up.

But where would we settle? While Dartmoor, and the ever-welcoming warmth of Sim's parents' cottage had so often felt like home to us over the past year, rental prices for a house large enough for the four of us locally were still far beyond our wildest budget. And when we looked at a map of the country, with very little to tie us to one place or another, and despite all our adventures in so many wild and beautiful places, it was the quiet corner of the Cotswolds we had left behind a year ago that called to us most strongly, that felt most like home. We had many emotional ties to that place – where Sim and I had first lived together, where both of our children had been born. I found myself daydreaming about the open fields, the ancient woods, the chalk grassland, the distant views of the plain and the downs and the miles of tranquil, wildlife-rich, traffic-free trails alongside the canal and river. It was also a place which would give us the ability to access everything we needed day-to-day without relying on a car, a huge concern for me.

Having wanted wildness and remoteness for so long, Sim and I had come to realise over our wild year even more strongly the value of connection, with people and places, for all of us. If it took another winter under canvas to make it a reality, it would be worth it.

Epilogue

WE FOUND OURSELVES, in that winter, adrift in a world that felt unsettled and unfamiliar. A world that, over the years that followed, would change beyond all recognition. We had always known we couldn't live wild forever, that we would need, eventually, to find somewhere more permanent. The past year and more had given us the foothold in the outdoor writing and photography industry that we needed. Buying a house was still – and would almost certainly always be – unimaginably far from our reach, but we could now pay rent without sacrificing all our time together.

We soon discovered, however, that our tattered credit rating made the normal channels of renting inaccessible to us. We searched endlessly for houses within our budget around the area where we wanted to be, contacting private landlords to see if they'd take us on and also asking everyone we knew. Finally, a wonderful woman came to our rescue, offering us the break we so needed. She was in the process of buying a small, terraced, ex-council house on the edge of town and was looking for tenants. She agreed that we could rent the house, initially for a much-reduced rent in return for our undertaking the renovation work it needed. It was exactly the stroke of luck we needed, but it would be the spring before the sale went through and we could move in.

The house had everything we were looking for: easy access to the countryside, a small garden with a tree big enough for the kids to climb, and a bright room that we could use as our office. It wasn't wild or remote, but it was within easy reach of a community, with shops and playgrounds a walk away. There were beautiful ancient woodlands with wych elms and beech trees, vast open chalk downland, rivers and fields nearby. There were no mountains, beaches or moorland but we would be within easy reach of many of our friends and family.

In some ways, knowing we would soon have a house to move into made the dark, damp days of our second winter under canvas even more difficult. Struggling to control our impatience to settle, we endured a difficult few months of living wild – travelling for work, camping whenever the weather allowed and staying with various family members, trying not to over-impose on any one household but often ending up at Sim's parents' tiny cottage. We will always be so grateful for their welcoming, accepting generosity during that time, and since, even when our mountain of stuff filled an entire room.

The reality was though, now we were no longer on a big adventure, we were simply homeless, in a winter of harsh storms far worse and far more frequent than those we had endured the previous year. The delightful freedom we had so embraced at the start of our year became, instead, a draining uncertainty and source of anxiety.

At long last, when I had almost stopped believing the house might ever happen, the time came for us to move in. Suddenly, there we were with rooms, walls, *space* – inside and out – of our own. It was almost funny how unused to it we were. Walking through the rooms of our small, terraced house, we wondered what we could possibly do with them all. The day we moved in I lay on the floor of the bright empty living room, overwhelmed with gratitude, bathing in the warm sunshine spilling through the windows – actual glass, double-glazed windows. At night we slept with those windows flung open wide, still struggling to adjust to the quiet, still air of indoors, ears straining to hear the calls of tawny owls from the nearby trees.

One of the strangest things about moving back into a house was the absolute ease of everything. Walking a few steps to the bathroom in the middle of the night, boiling a kettle at the flick of a switch, filling the fridge with perishables, running a bath with hot water and stepping into it in complete privacy – well, whatever the equivalent is with two young children about. All these things felt alien, almost to the point where I felt guilty about doing them for a brief moment before the realisation struck that it was just *normal*. Still, I sometimes felt we were missing out on something, missing out on the raw realness of the routines of that wild year. In many ways, it was the effort required to eat, drink, wash, entertain that had made the end result so special. Without that, it lost some of its richness. Our trip had taught

...eep joy to be found in the simple acts of everyday
...d value in taking time and care over them.

...many ways our wild year made me tougher – certainly,
...ore resilient to physical hardship. In other ways it made
me appreciate the softer, gentler things – warmth, rest, health
– all the more. Even my long-term love of running changed.
Whereas, in my comfortable, pre-child days I actively sought
pain and discomfort, accepting actual damage to my body as
a payoff for the brief moments of mental calm that extreme
endurance challenges brought me, now I found this reversed.
I now recognise it's important not to exhaust myself on every
run – so I can still be the best possible version of myself, for my
children, Sim and our work.

There are so many things we didn't know when we started
our year of camping, things we had to learn quickly, from the
limitations of our kit, and those of ourselves, to the difficulties
of finding a good laundrette in rural Britain. But we learnt so
many positive lessons, too. That being together, being guided by
our children as we, in turn, attempt to guide them through the
foundations of their lives, is not just important, but essential.
That it is possible, even if it does take some fairly drastic
measures, to live a more shared, more equal life. One that,
rather than being compartmentalised into work, relationships,
parenting and play is all part of one noisy, messy, busy and yet
incredibly fulfilling existence.

E and H are growing up, discovering their rapidly unfolding
worlds, learning, testing, playing, caring as they go. They both
play music, which fills my heart with joy. And they're both
passionate and steadfast in their roles as protectors of wild places

and wild things. Their growing independence also means Sim and I sometimes get to go running together, rather than always having to take it in turns as we did in the past.

In the end, our trusty truck bowed out right on cue, succumbing to its pervasive rust and failing its MOT. Having bought it out of necessity when we gave up our house, it had looked after us impeccably through the weather and the miles, over the rough and the smooth. Sitting high up in the cab, all our possessions packed into the leaky load bay at the back, it felt like the right vehicle for our adventures: as safe as we could afford, rugged and capable enough for wherever we chose to go, and with plenty of space for us all. For the whole time we were houseless, the truck was our constant companion. Once it even helped to pull some shiny new campervans out of a muddy Devon campsite. Much as we would have loved to have bought a less polluting vehicle, this just wasn't possible on our budget – so we tried always to drive it as little as we could, while still seeing many of Britain's beautiful places and travelling as far as we needed to for work. We had planned to sell it anyway, having moved somewhere where it was no longer necessary, but instead it went for spare parts, continuing to be useful even in its afterlife.

Money is still hard, and the future might always be uncertain, but right now our life is financially sustainable, something we wondered whether was possible when we first set out and, indeed, at certain points of our wild year. Bankruptcy, though still hard to say and difficult to look back on, did, in the end, free us from debts that would have dragged us so far down we may never have got back up again. We relish working for ourselves and have now written several guidebooks, which we hope might inspire someone else to step outside into the unknown and have amazing adventures, big or small. Creating each book is a bit like living our wild year over again, experiencing the highs and lows, successes and failures, making those essential human connections and coming out the other side stronger in our partnership, with many lessons learnt. Savings, in the way of so many of our generation, are an impossible dream. We still have nothing to fall back on should we stumble upon hard times again, but we do have plenty of camping kit and we're not afraid to use it. We also know now that home really can be wherever we pitch it.

And what of our earthly home – our natural world, our National Parks, Areas of Outstanding Natural Beauty, and our escalating climate crisis? Rewilding Britain is campaigning for wilder National Parks, calling on the UK Government and devolved administrations to restore wildness and biodiversity; to prioritise nurturing nature-depleted Britain back to health. Ever more extreme weather and natural disasters are hammering the message home to even those who deny there's a problem that, as a species, we cannot continue living this way. Ultimately, it is those few who hold the most power who have the greatest ability to effect real, meaningful, lasting change. But, sharing this planet that is the only place we can exist, we must all do our bit, considering where we invest our money from the food we buy to the banks and utilities companies we support. And, for those who choose to bring children into the world, raising the next generation in a way that cares deeply for the natural world, and understands its inextricable link to the surviving and thriving of human beings.

Every day, as we work for ourselves, raise our children and share everything in our lives equally, we know that this was what we were aiming for when we took that giant leap into the unknown. And we are so glad we did, because the precious wild places we visited may not be around for ever, and our children will, one day in the not-too-distant future, leave us behind to pursue their own lives. But we know that, from the day we set out and right now at this moment, we are wholeheartedly experiencing life together.

It's taken me five years since we returned to a more 'normal' way of life to feel ready to write this book. I wanted to gather the words and photographs and memories of our wild year so that it would exist at least for E and H, who were so young at the time, to read should they, one day, want to know more about the time we went and lived in a tent. For Sim and me, there is no chance we will forget: it was a time unlike any other in our lives. One that changed everything.

kit list for a wild year

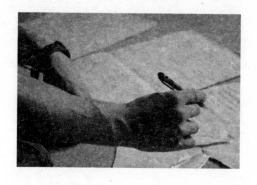

Soulpad bell tent

Tent carpet, tarp and inner tent

Stores: double burner, Frontier, Jetboil

Kelly kettle

Backpacking tent

Mattresses and bedding

Camping mats and sleeping bags

Clothing

Waterproof duffle bags

Day pack

Child carriers

Head torch and USB lantern

Mugs, bowls, cutlery, pans and steamer

Washbag and baby changing

Food staples

Penknife, multitool and axe

Boots, wellies and running shoes

Foldable kids' bath

Smart clothes - one set each

Large waterproof boxes

Camera, laptop and phones

Binoculars

Chargers and cables

Toys and books

Guidebooks, maps and compass

Box of Wild Running books

Coffee grinder and press

First aid kit

Lightweight table and chairs

Convection heater

Solar shower

Water filter

Credits

Page vii extracted from *Walden* by Henry David Thoreau, 1854.

Page 35 extracted from *The Great Gatsby* by F. Scott Fitzgerald, 1925.

Page 91 extracted from *The Letters of Emily Dickinson* by Emily Dickinson, 1895.

Page 119 extracted from *Walden* by Henry David Thoreau, 1854.

Page 131 extracted from *The Sense of Wonder* by Rachel Carson, 1965.

Page 179 extracted from *The Letters of Robert Browning and Elizabeth Barret Barrett 1845-1846 Vol I* by Elizabeth Barrett Browning.

Page 219 extracted from *Virginia Woolf, A Passionate Apprentice: The Early Journals, 1897-1909*.

Page 222 extracted from *Lorna Doone* by R.D. Blackmore, 1869.

Photography throughout the book by Jen & Sim Benson.

Acknowledgements

With all my heart, thank you to Sim, E and H for the joy of sharing the adventure that is our everyday.

From both of us, our love and thanks to our families for always being there for us, even at 3am with a truck full of wet tent.

A huge thank you to Katie Bond for belief in, and enthusiasm for, our books over the years, and to Phoebe Bath, Viviane Basset and all the team at Aurum and Quarto. Thank you to Victoria Millar for insightful, thoughtful and patient editing; Anna Morrison for summing up our wild year in one incredibly beautiful cover; Aruna Vasudevan and Lesley Malkin for invaluable and eagle-eyed input; and Claire Maxwell for sharing our story.

Our heartfelt thanks to all those who offered us friendship, kindness and support throughout our wild year and beyond, including: Wild Things Daniel, Tania and Rose; Sarah Churchill; Elaine Wainwright & family; James, Monika & Zuza; Christine & Gavin; Ros Shuttleworth; Jimmy, Sara & family; Zoe & Mark Vanderstay; Bell Tent UK; Taunton Leisure; Nick & Helen Baron; Collette Pryer & family; Andy, Sandy & family; The Meek family; Alpkit; Charlie Friday's in Lynton; Hook Farm campsite; Eskdale and Great Langdale campsites; Town Mill Bakery; Rob Joules; Liz Multon; Peter Taylor; Renee McGregor; and the Taylor and McGrogan families. Thanks to the teams at *Walk*, *Trail Running*, *Trail* and *Country Walking* magazines and to former editors Amy Curtis and Claire Maxted.

Lastly, many thanks to the incredible organisations we've been proud and honoured to work with, including Ordnance Survey and the GetOutside team, the National Trust, the Wildlife Trusts, and YHA.